Stealth Confiscation

Compliments of
Randy Hillier, MPP
Lanark-Frontenac-Lennox and
Addington

"*Traditional legal thinkers in both the Roman law and common law tradition consistently insisted on this key proposition: 'property is the guardian of every other right.' The logic that drives this expression is that only a system of private property lets people form and raise families, organize religious and other charitable organizations, and earn a living through honest labour.*"
—Professor Richard Epstein, in *Supreme Neglect* (2008: 2)

Stealth Confiscation

How governments regulate, freeze
and devalue private property—
without compensation

Mark Milke

The Fraser Institute
2012

Date of issue: May 2012

Printed and bound in Canada

Editing: Kristin McCahon

Typesetting and design: Lindsey Thomas Martin

Cover design and artwork: Bill C. Ray

National Library of Canada Cataloguing in Publication Data

Stealth Confiscation: How Governments Regulate, Freeze And Devalue Private Property—without Compensation / by Mark Milke

Includes bibliographical references.

ISBN 978-0-88975-256-6.

Contents

Overview

"Among the 13 countries, Canada ranks as offering the lowest degree of compensation rights."
—Rachelle Alterman, in *Takings International* (2010: 3)

Regulatory takings—stealth expropriation by another name and without compensation

In Canada, the principle of compensation for expropriation of property is well-established. Tradition, well-established common law principles, laws (including much provincial legislation that requires compensation for expropriation) and court rulings that reinforce the same are available to property owners who face a threat of unusable (and therefore devalued) property.

However, unlike expropriation, regulatory changes that restrict the use of property (and can affect its value) rarely result in compensation in Canada, in contrast to other developed countries. In Canada, governments can and do restrict the use of property to such an extent that the action is akin to expropriation. Such regulatory takings can occur via laws and regulatory changes by all levels of government. There is thus a substantial need for public policy to fill the gap for those affected by regulatory takings, while still recognizing the public interest element whereby governments will, on occasion, need to expropriate and regulate property.

Four examples (expanded on in the main section of this book and with additional examples then provided) make clear the need for reforms in this increasingly used form of takings.

A three-decade regulatory freeze in Alberta

In 1976, Bill Nilsson, a farmer near Edmonton with 160 acres, applied to the Ministry of the Environment in order to obtain permission to build a mobile home park on part of his property. Permission was necessary due to a 1974 decision by the province to create the North Edmonton Restricted Development Area (RDA), a designation that, as the name implies, restricted development without permission from the province (see the main body of this paper for legal and other references). In response to his application, the government of Alberta refused permission, and publicly asserted the land was to be preserved for use as a greenbelt or parkland at some future date. Given that he could not develop his property, Nilsson considered selling it to the government. However, the province's tender was for only $2,500 an acre, compared to a government purchase price of $10,000 per acre for land on either side of his property. Nilsson refused.

Negotiations continued and by the recession in the early 1980s, Nilsson agreed to sell at the initial offered price on the condition he retain the right to appeal to the Land Compensation Board. That same board later awarded Nilsson $15,000 per acre. The provincial government refused to pay and went to court. Nilsson won at the Court of Queen's Bench where he was awarded $9.1 million in principal and compound interest, as well as costs. He won again at the Court of Appeal. However, the government continued to appeal the case to the Supreme Court of Canada. In 2003 that court refused to hear the province's appeal, thus allowing the lower court rulings and monetary compensation to stand.

In court proceedings, it was discovered that the original justification for the Restricted Development Area and the subsequent denial of the proposed trailer park development—a greenbelt designation—was never true. Instead, the province wanted Nilsson's land for an eventual ring road and utility corridor, facts that did not surface until evidence was presented in court years later. The Alberta government lied about the reason for the regulation of Nilsson's land for a simple reason: assigning his land as a future highway and utility corridor would have triggered expropriation statutes including much higher compensation.

In this case, it is useful to note that had the province of Alberta wanted Nilsson's land for its stated purpose—a greenbelt or parkland—Nilsson would not have been able to obtain full compensation for the government-imposed regulatory loss. The Nilsson case points to the clear need for regulatory actions to be converted to akin-to-expropriation actions in order to give property owners just compensation.

How regulation made Coquitlam private property "sterile"

In 2005, the City of Coquitlam, British Columbia, widened a local road which in turn caused a nearby creek to encroach upon a privately-owned 1.5 acre parcel of land. In addition, the city declared a seepage ditch in the centre of the property (and which contained only mud and not flowing water) to be a fish habitat. That designation also meant the land also came under provincial and federal jurisdiction, this despite the fact, as the owner noted, it was a mere trickle and could never support fish.

The declaration of a fish habitat, combined with increased 24-metre setbacks for the road, led the entire 1.5 acre parcel to be declared "sterile" by the city. That designation meant no development could occur, and the land that previously could have been subdivided into ten lots thus became worth little in practical terms.

The 1.5 acre parcel was owned for 18 years by Barry and Linda Sheridan of Coquitlam. They planned to subdivide the land and use the proceeds to fund their retirement. The Sheridans were eventually successful in convincing the City of Coquitlam to re-zone the land for a ten-lot housing development. However, that only occurred after the Sheridans hired their own Qualified Environmental Professional (QEP) to analyze the land in question at a substantial cost to themselves. Had they not been successful, the regulations applied to their land would have severely restricted its use and severely devalued it.

Regulatory freezing—CPR, Vancouver, and the Arbutus Corridor

In the year 2000, the City of Vancouver passed a bylaw to declare a 22 kilometre-long corridor as a public thoroughfare for transportation, including rail and a "greenway" with public walks, nature trails, and cycle paths. The land had been owned and managed by the Canadian Pacific Railway (CPR) since 1886. The effect of the bylaw, as the Supreme Court wrote later, "was to freeze the redevelopment potential of the corridor and to confine CPR to uneconomic uses of the land."

The city offered CPR no compensation. The city also made it clear that it would not purchase the land. CPR's view, as described in court documents, was that it was "intolerable" for the city to seek to keep the land intact without purchasing it. Still, the Supreme Court of Canada ruled in the city's favour.

Ontario's wetlands designations and subsequent loss of value

In Ontario, the province can designate marshes, bogs, swamps, and fens (wetlands that accumulate peat) as "Provincially Significant Wetlands." Under the Conservation Authorities Act, local municipalities must comply with such a designation. Also, even "basic wetland" (not initially considered provincially significant) can later be affected through a regulations permit process called "complexing," which allows basic wetland to be designated "provincially significant" if it is within 750 metres of an existing Provincially Significant Wetland.

In one example from Ottawa, Tony Walker, head of the Goulbourn Landowners Group, described the effect of provincial wetlands designation combined with subsequent city zoning on the local property owners: "Affected landowners were not informed that they are in the buffer zone, or of the restrictions on their property." At the end of it all said Walker, "The city stated that it does not intend to compensate landowners for the devaluation of their properties. The effect of these designations is to devalue and freeze private property."

The problem in a nutshell

Even where governments are found to be *legally* in the right, as in *CPR. v. Vancouver*, such rulings do not remove the real-world effect of private land frozen and instead used for public purposes and without compensation.

The relevant question is not whether governments ought to regulate property in some minimalist fashion—they surely will (see Epstein, 2005, for a more detailed discussion)—but how. After all, in private disputes, homeowners possess some recourse rights if another private party interferes in that homeowner's use of their property (the tort of nuisance).[1] This is one core problem with having no liability rule for regulatory takings: it allows governments to impair rights of use with impunity, while private individuals are liable in nuisance cases for impairing just such rights. Thus,

---

1 The tort of nuisance is "a protection against being unlawfully annoyed, prejudiced or disturbed in the enjoyment of land" (Heuston, 1977: 50).

the same state that prevents such private interference via a legal framework should also apply the same standard to itself—and beyond just existing expropriation provisions—to include public regulatory takings.

The case for compensation
There is an obvious loss of use (and value)
In a 2008 report from the David Suzuki Foundation on BC's Agricultural Land Reserve (ALR), the report made no mention of the need to compensate property owners for land frozen for agricultural use only. But the Foundation explicitly acknowledged the loss of use (and thus of value), when it noted a substantial differential in price in farmland in the Fraser Valley.

Even foreign companies are treated better than our own
The University of Alberta's Russell Brown has noted that under Article 1110 of NAFTA, investors from the United States or Mexico with holdings in Canada may initiate a claim to determine whether Canada has imposed a "measure" that is "tantamount to... expropriation, thereby triggering a right in the investor to compensation." Importantly as well, the same argument applies to all offshore investors from counterpart states under the dozens of free trade agreements and Foreign Investment Promotion and Protection Agreements (FIPAs) into which Canada has entered. As Brown points out, "all FIPAs to which Canada is a party effectively preclude the parties' ability to take except where the taking is for a public purpose, effected under due process of law, non-discriminatory and compensated."

Canada fares poorly in international compensation comparisons
Canada's non-compensation for regulatory takings sets it apart from other major Western countries. In a survey of 13 nations, Canada and Australia are the most restrictive about compensating for regulatory takings. As Rachelle Alterman writes in her introduction to the survey, "Among the 13 countries, Canada ranks as offering the lowest degree of compensation rights" including major takings, direct partial takings, and indirect partial takings. In contrast, Poland, Germany, Sweden, Israel, and the Netherlands all provide the broadest compensation rights as it concerns major regulatory takings.

For example, Poland has a special remedy whereby land designated for public use but not taken (expropriated with compensation) within a reasonable time allows a landowner to force the government to expropriate—far preferable to waiting for regulatory compensation. Similarly, in Germany and Sweden, property owners can initiate a "transfer-of-title" claim if regulatory actions are delayed.

Governments in Israel and the Netherlands, for unique reasons, often designate a plot of land for public purposes in advance of expropriation. That regulatory designation, though, can and does trigger a two-part process for compensation: first, compensation due to the restricted use and accompanying loss of value of the land; and second, compensation for the remaining value once expropriated. Critically for property owners, this means that regulation cannot be used to deny any and all compensation; the regulatory action *itself* triggers compensation.

Beyond the individual examples, the European Union generally has strong protection of property rights compared to Canada, which has led Alterman to comment that "Had Canada been in Europe, some aspects of its law on major takings may not have survived ECHR [European Commission on Human Rights] scrutiny."

Recommendations

The reluctance, and in some cases the straightforward unwillingness of governments to compensate Canadians for regulatory infringements on their property is an omission that needs to be rectified. Justifications are not difficult to find: regulations that substantially or wholly restrict the use of property are little different from expropriation in that they also literally remove the use of property. Thus, this paper recommends the following broad principle: treat regulatory takings akin to expropriation takings. Five specific recommendations then follow from that principle.

Broad recommendation—treat regulatory takings as akin to expropriation

This broad recommendation stems from the example and practice in selected countries that see little or no difference between a loss of use and value of property that stem from acts of expropriation or acts of regulation that effect major takings. Germany, Israel and the Netherlands are models to follow here. In particular, note how Gerd Schmidt-Eichstaedt describes the German approach to regulatory takings:

The German law of liability for damages caused by planning decisions (*Planungsschadensrecht*) is concerned with compensating property owners for the effects of (lawful) interferences by public authorities with their property rights. In German legal doctrine, it is irrelevant whether liability for damages is caused by an expropriation decision within the meaning of article 14 of the Basic Law or by a regulation that restricts property rights. In the end, they are always a form of property restriction … .

The whole or partial loss of use of property and the often subsequent decline in value of property due to regulation for a public end demands compensation on the principle that where governments wish private property for public purposes, the public should bear the cost of that designation, not individual property holders.

Actionable recommendation 1

Canadian governments should follow the example of Germany, Israel, the Netherlands, Poland, and Sweden and fully compensate property owners for major takings (as these five countries do) and direct partial takings (as Israel and the Netherlands do), and to a lesser and limited degree, indirect partial takings.

Rationale

In order to treat regulatory takings as akin to expropriation, it should be assumed as part of the regulatory and planning processes that major takings and direct partial takings will be compensated. Indirect partial takings will need to be compensated on more restricted grounds, but should also be considered where use has been restricted by regulations or planning and property values harmed as a result.

Actionable recommendation 2

Allow property owners to convert major regulatory takings and direct partial takings into expropriation actions.

Rationale

Where a regulatory or planning action has limited the use of all or portions of a property, federal and provincial law (including municipal law for which provinces are responsible), should allow the property owner to demand title transfer in order to convert a regulatory action into an expropriation action, which would then trigger compensation. This is based on the German and Swedish model for major takings but is extended here for direct partial takings.

Actionable recommendation 3

In the case of partial direct takings and as regards compensation, the decrease or increase in value should be defined in a net manner. Doing so would take into account both the harm a regulatory action caused to one part of a property, which might cause it to lose value, and the benefits a regulatory action caused to another part of the property, which might increase its value.

Rationale

In terms of value, both the harm and benefit to the use of a property (and then the value reduction or increase) should be calculated on a net basis. After all, if a city designates part of a piece of farmland for a future industrial park and thus raises its value, it is reasonable to count that new use and increase in property value against any negative regulatory takings to arrive at a net compensation figure. This follows on the German model.

Actionable recommendation 4

Compensation levels should account for the effect of the old regulation versus the new regulation and difference between old and new plans.

Rationale

In the case of regulation or land planning changes, a determination should be made as to whether the old regulation or old and new land planning designation is any more or less harmful to value than the new regulation. This would avoid specious claims and follow on the German model.

Actionable recommendation 5

When property use is newly restricted, compensation should be offered where the value of property has fallen 5 percent or more as a result of the change in regulation or plans.

Rationale

Poland compensates for takings "at the first zloty" whereas Israel compensates where a decline in property values has been greater than 1 to 3 percent. In a recent court case in Finland, property owners unable to cut down trees for their forestry business were compensated when restricted use of their land meant its value had declined by 4 percent. In the United States, depending on the court judgment or the state in question, losses must be severely high, 100 percent in some cases, before compensation for regulatory harm can be claimed.

The American model is the outlier and Canada should follow the European guidelines and compensate when usage has led to a decline in property values of 5 percent or more.

Stealth Confiscation

Property rights defined

"In 1969, as prime minister, Mr. Trudeau again proposed entrenchment of a charter of rights which would have guaranteed the right of an individual to use and enjoy property, with the assurance that there would be no deprivation of property except in accordance with proper legal procedures."
—The Library of Parliament, describing Pierre Trudeau's initial attempts to inject property rights into Canada's Constitution (Johansen, 1991).

What is property?

Property can be defined in three broad ways: two that are more "traditional" and one that is conceptually newer. In general, "traditional" types of property consist of rights in real property (land and buildings) and personal property (chattels and intangible forms of property) such as shares and negotiable instruments.

Additionally, and related to the first categorization is a second type: intellectual property. This type includes copyright and patent protection as examples. However, this is also intangible property, and is different from the first type in that it is purely a creation of statute. In this latter case, the federal government through the Canadian Intellectual Property Office defines intellectual property as "Legal rights that result from intellectual activity in the industrial, scientific, literary and artistic fields" (Canada, undated).

Alternatively, and thirdly, is some attempt to expand the definition of property to government disbursements such as welfare payments, old age benefits, and unemployment compensation (Johansen, 1991). However, as a working definition, this book will use the first and second conceptions of property—real property and intellectual property—and for the following reasons:

1. First, real property and intellectual property are both examples of property that can be created or purchased by individuals. As will be explained more fully in the addendum on the history of property rights, it is why John Locke asserted that private property and associated rights matter: because one's labour (or that of one's ancestors) is key to the creation of such private property (Locke, 1690/1997: 18). For example, the picking of berries on an open public field makes those berries the property of the person who picked them and that person can then consume, give away, or sell such fruit.

    In the case of intellectual property, the software designer's labour was involved in the creation of a program and thus it is the designer's right to profit from her labour. The initial labour thus creates a right to property over and above all other claimants. (That noted, while intellectual property is defensible as akin to real property, this book will focus on regulatory takings only as they apply to real property, this for the sake of clarity in recommended legislative reforms.)

2. Second, and in contrast, the attempt to claim that benefits from the state also constitute "property" is an attempt to corral the fruit of the labour of others and turn that claim into a right. A social program or a welfare benefit may be useful or ill-advised, superior or poor social policy, or some descriptor in between. But in every instance, taxpayer-funded programs are clearly the result of the efforts of other people, who first work with their own labour (physical or mental), and then who pay taxes. Clearly, a portion of their labour has been taken from them and delivered to another person.

3. Third, in general, it may be desirable for an orchardist through a voluntary gift to the poor, or more indirectly through taxes, to share part of her apple harvest, but it is clear that her labour has been given or taken for the sustenance of others. Thus, to claim someone else's labour is property to which one is entitled to protection under the law, is to place that working person's labour involuntarily in the service of others. No "right" can reasonably be asserted to the product of someone else's labour, even where in selected circumstances such takings may be desirable and justifiable. Such takings can still occur without turning them into a right.

Property as a right

If property as a right is created by labour, what more specifically does that right entail? Bryce Wilkinson summarizes property rights as "the formal and informal rules that govern access to and use of property."[1] He notes that ownership of title is only one aspect of property rights. The ability to use the property is key. Without it, the ability to derive income from the property (e.g., to rent or profit from crops on said land); to dispose of the property (e.g., destroy, sell, or otherwise alienate it); and exclude others, thus permitting the quiet enjoyment of one's property, can all be impaired (Wilkinson, 2008: 8).

Rainer Knopff asserts that while allowing that acquisition and possession cannot be entirely separated—"if possession is insecure, one of the most powerful incentives for acquisition is removed"—he nonetheless notes that property rights are "more rights of acquisition than of possession or consumption" (Knopff, 2002: 50).

Both Knopff and Wilkinson thus identify a key component of property rights: it is not enough to merely possess property; one must also be able to *do* something with it—to use it in some manner if one is so inclined. Both thus hint at why property rights are important to begin with and which leads to a consideration of two justifications for why protection of private property is critical.

Why are property rights important? The functional case for protection

The case for protection of property can be justified on a moral or a functional basis. An example of the moral justification is found in the 1789 *Declaration of the Rights of Man and of the Citizen*. There, the French

---

1   Thus, what is at stake in regulation, then, is the right of use (and not necessarily the value of the property, though that will be affected by restrictions on use). The difference may be explained in this manner: I don't have a guaranteed right to a particular property value. For example, if someone's lawful use of their property results in a devaluation of my own property, I cannot sue for the loss of value. I can, however, sue them if their otherwise lawful use of their property impairs my *use* of my own property. That's the same right—use—that is impaired by a public authority exercising its otherwise lawful rights of regulation. It is land use regulation, and not land value that is at issue. The value of the property, while important, is the secondary effect.

revolutionaries asserted in Article 17 that "Since the right to Property is inviolable and sacred, no one may be deprived thereof, unless public necessity, legally ascertained, obviously requires it, and just and prior indemnity has been paid" (France, 1789).

Similarly, Locke asserted that private property and associated rights matter because one's labour, or one's ancestors' labour, was used to create such private property (Locke, 1690/1997: 18). Those who pick the berries on an open, public field make those berries their property by the act of picking them. The act of labour has, in theory, created a right, a right to property that now excludes others from one's newly acquired fruit.

On the functional side, Knopff, while drawing on the theoretical work of Montesquieu and Locke, notes the point of property rights: "to fuel the acquisitive engine at the heart of the capitalist system, so as to generate surplus wealth and reinvestment, thus enlarging the economic pie of both rich and poor" (2002: 50). Similarly, James Gwartney et al. argue that "Protection of persons and their rightfully acquired property is a central element of economic freedom and a civil society. Indeed, it is the most important function of government ..." (Gwartney et al., 2011: 3–5).

University of Chicago law professor and constitutional scholar Richard Epstein gives a detailed elaboration of the functional benefits of property rights. He explains that theorists, including Hugo Grotius, John Locke, and Adam Smith, used variations of the moral argument. Grotius thought all persons consented to a "first taker" rule that was self-evident (i.e., land belongs to the first person who settles it, for example, or, in another example, an inventor has the right to the patent on his product and to benefit from the invention for a period of time). Smith asserted that an impartial observer would recognize the special position of the first taker. Epstein says that instead, the strength of a claim to private property and the protection of the same "rested on its productive advantage and not merely on an obscure natural law claim that property rights are necessarily 'immutable' across all times and places" (2008: 18–19).

Epstein further notes that "the true genius of property rights is in how they facilitate more complex forms of both joint control *and* divided control of resources. Both allow for specialization and cooperation between persons" (2008: 20). He notes the example of land pooled with others' where a partnership could lease for terms of years rather than selling it, or they could place a mortgage upon it, as security for a loan. In these and multiple other examples, the clear recording of property rights, the multiple interests sometimes contained therein, and enforcement of the same allow stability between trading partners and a notice to the greater world about who "is in a position to sell, mortgage or lease it ... In so doing, the recording system increases the gains from trade by preventing double-dealing" (2008: 21).

Similarly, Hernando de Soto discusses the functional effect of property rights and gives clear examples as to their utility:

> Look around: everything of economic value that you own—house and car titles, mortgages, checking accounts, stocks, contracts, patents, other people's debts (including derivatives)—is documented on paper. You are able to hold, transfer, assess, and certify the value of such assets only through documents that have been legally authenticated by a global system of rules, procedures, and standards. Ensuring that the relationship between those documents and each of the independent assets they represent is never debased requires a formidable system of legal property rights. That system produces the trust that allows credit and capital to flow and markets to work. (de Soto, 2009, February 21: 1)

A question should naturally arise at this point: What happens when the system of property rights and protection of the same does not work, and does not allow credit and capital to flow, and this because of a relatively new interference in the use of one's property—something known as "regulatory takings"? I discuss this problem next.

CHAPTER ONE

Property rights problems in Canada

> *"No land use law in the world can evade the need to address the relationship between land use regulation and property values."*
> —Rachelle Alterman, in *Takings International* (2010: 3)

A definition of regulatory takings

By "regulatory taking" I am describing how government regulation can and does restrict the use of property to such an extent that such actions are akin to expropriation. I will use the term "regulatory takings" to describe the action or concept, but it is also known by other designations including "constructive expropriation," "*de facto* taking," "*de facto* expropriation," "planning expropriation" and "material expropriation" (Alterman, 2010: 23). "Constructive taking" is another way of describing it. For example, University of Alberta Law professor Russell Brown prefers "constructive taking" as that term is "more precisely descriptive of the legal effect—itself a 'judicial construct'—ascribed to the public authority's conduct" (2007: 316).

For the purpose of this paper though, I use "regulatory taking," as it has the advantage that it clearly informs the reader that I will address *regulatory actions by governments* that affect the use of property to such an extent to be akin to whole or partial expropriation. If a government or a bureaucracy freezes all or part of your property, they have, for all intents and purposes, "taken" it. Such an action can fairly be described, then, as a regulatory taking.

Why regulatory takings are the newest problem for property owners

In contrast to expropriation, and as it regards zoning regulations, in E.C.E. Todd's *Law of Expropriation and Compensation in Canada*, the author summarizes the current state whereby governments are not obligated to pay compensation for matters related to regulation:

> By the imposition, removal, or alteration of land use controls a public authority may dramatically increase, or decrease, the value of land by changing the permitted uses which may be made of it. In such a case, in the absence of express statutory provision to the contrary an owner is not entitled to compensation or other remedy notwithstanding that subdivision approval or rezoning is refused or development is blocked or frozen pursuant to statutory planning powers in order, for example, to facilitate the future acquisition of the land for public purposes. (Todd, 1992: 22–23)

As Epstein points out with reference to the United States, modern constitutional law and interpretation tends to treat the property as the important "thing," with the exclusion of use, clearly ordered or *de facto* engendered, as secondary and of little importance: "It is as though the holder of an orange is entitled to exclusive possession of the rind, but needs government permission to use or dispose of the fruit that lies within" (2008: xvi).

Given the labour that goes into the creation of private property and its functional benefits, the onus must be on government to demonstrate why a regulatory interference with property is warranted and reasonable. If the onus was instead on the property owner, the point of assumed rights would be turned on its head: the owner would be forced to fend off any and all attempts by government at interference as if the burden of proof lay with the private property owner. Practically speaking, it would be a rather ill-matched contest given the resources of government vis-à-vis all but the very wealthiest of individuals or corporations (and even then, as *CPR v. Vancouver (2006)* will shortly show, there is no guarantee that one can "beat" City Hall).

The reasoning here in favour of requiring governments to justify takings is thus similar to the section 1 test in the *Canadian Charter of Rights and Freedoms*. Section 1 states: "The *Canadian Charter of Rights and Freedoms* guarantees the rights and freedoms set out in it subject only to such reasonable limits prescribed by law as can be demonstrably justified in a free and democratic society" (Canada, 1982). In the 1986 case *R. v. Oakes*, the

Supreme Court of Canada ruled that the onus is on the government to prove that any restrictions on rights and freedoms are indeed reasonable.

Regulation is assumed; the relevant question is what to compensate and for how much

The onus put upon governments then assumes some interference with private property will always occur—but that it must be properly circumscribed, justified, and compensated. On that assumption, the case for assuming some regulation of property (including expropriation with compensation for wider public interest reasons) is not unusual in the history of property rights.[1] Epstein in his discussion of social contract theory notes that "sound government requires each person to forfeit some fraction of his liberty and property to supply the state with the authority and resources needed to enforce prior entitlements to liberty and property" (2008: 29). Knopff points out that as important as property is, "it has never been considered an absolute right in the liberal tradition," and some allowance for governments to regulate or expropriate property has thus always been made, "though early liberal theorists such as Locke and Montesquieu established a strong presumption against it" (2002: 50).

---

1   Moreover, it should be noted that a sort of "*quid pro quo*" exists between property owners and government. Property owners also benefit from government actions, such as when a public park is created near their property that increases the value of the private land. In such cases, owners are not required to compensate government when a regulatory change *increases* the value of their land. Just as on the one hand it would be unreasonable to expect a property owner to suffer the loss of a significant portion of the value of his or her land, it would also be unreasonable to expect quite minor losses through justifiable and necessary regulation to always be compensated for—and precisely because some free benefits also accrue to property owners. Just as it would be unreasonable to expect a homeowner who benefits from a new park nearby to pay compensation to government for said benefit, it is reasonable to assert in reverse that minor infringements are justifiable as perfect remedies are not usually available. Obviously, the useful concepts here, impossible as they are to define with perfect precision, are reasonableness and proportion. Property owners and governments should both have the expectation of reasonableness from each other. In severe differences as to what constitutes "reasonable," owners do have access to litigation, but as will be demonstrated, this is of little help in Canada at present on the question of regulatory takings. This paper aims in part to help clarify what constitutes a reasonable taking versus an unreasonable taking and suggests legal and constitutional remedies to that end.

Historically, case law on the question of regulation has reached the same conclusions. Consider *France Fenwick & Co. v. The King* (1927): "A mere negative prohibition though it involves interference with an owner's enjoyment of property, does not, I think, merely because it is obeyed, carry with it at common law any right to compensation" (*Fenwick*, supra, at 467). In *Belfast Corporation v. O. D. Cars Ltd.* (1960), where the respondent sought, and was denied, a development permit for the erection of industrial and commercial premises on its property, Lord Radcliffe noted that

> from the earliest of times the owner of property, and in particular of land, has been restricted in his free enjoyment of it not only by the common law maxim *sic utere tuo ut alienum non laedas* [use your own property so as not to injure that of another], but by positive enactments limiting his use or even imposing burdens upon him. (*Belfast Corporation v. O. D. Cars Ltd.* (1960), supra, at 523)

Lord Radcliffe also remarked how "during the second half of the nineteenth century came the great movement for the regulation of life in cities and towns in the interests of public health and amenity." Also, "Generally speaking, though not without exception, these obligations and restrictions were treated as not requiring compensation, though, of course, in a sense they expropriated certain rights of property." Critical to note as regards compensation, "the consequent control, impairment, or diminution of those rights was not treated as a 'taking' of property nor, when compensation was provided, was it provided on the basis that property or property rights had been 'taken,' *but on the basis that property, itself retained, had been injuriously affected*" (*Belfast Corporation v. O. D. Cars Ltd.*, 1960, supra, at 523) (emphasis added).

Thus, the relevant question for anyone concerned with preserving the rights to the use of property and the attendant benefits that flow from it to individuals, families, and society is not whether governments ought to regulate property in some minimalist fashion—they surely will—but how.

The private sector couldn't act like this ...

In personal affairs, a homeowner would likely object if her next door neighbour set up a meat-packing plant replete with smells, even if harmless. The objection would likely be that both the use and value of her own property would be impaired. Few people would care to spend much time outdoors on their patio if the smell of a meat-packing plant wafted by; that would also likely lead to devalued property. The homeowner might well seek recourse in nuisance law whereby private actors cannot impair the use and enjoyment of others' property.

This then makes obvious a double-standard whereby the state is able to engage in an act that significantly restricts the use of one's property while (more properly) restricting such actions when performed by private parties. In private affairs, Party A cannot impair, with impunity, the rights of use that Party B has in his or her property. Moreover, the state constitutes courts to ensure that those rights of use, and the corresponding rights to compensation where rights of use are impaired, are respected. And yet, that same state does not apply those liabilities, to which it subjects Party A, to itself.

This problem of takings is clear in the case of expropriation. There, in jurisdictions that respect the rule of law, fair compensation must be offered unless the clearest statement to the contrary displaces the common law presumption that Parliament or the legislature intended to compensate for a taking. Traditionally, Canada's courts understand this and have reaffirmed the principle of compensation in cases of expropriation. For example, in *Toronto Area Transit Operating Authority v. Dell Holdings Ltd.* (1997), the Supreme Court of Canada wrote that,

> The expropriation of property is one of the ultimate exercises of governmental authority. To take all or part of a person's property constitutes a severe loss and a very significant interference with a citizen's private property rights. It follows that the power of an expropriating authority should be strictly construed in favour of those whose rights have been affected. This principle has been stressed by eminent writers and emphasized in decisions of this Court. (*Toronto Area Transit Operating Authority v. Dell Holdings Ltd.* (1997))

Thus, as regards expropriation, the courts have generally found that some level of compensation is due. However, more recently, the problem of regulatory takings has arisen whereby regulatory changes can have the same end effect as expropriation, except with the important distinction that the regulatory taking is not accompanied by compensation. Examples of just such takings are provided next.

CHAPTER TWO

Examples of significant regulatory takings

"We do not exclude the possibility that in an exceptional case the nature or extent of restrictions imposed on land use might be so significant that a de facto taking of the property has occurred."
—The Court of Appeal of Alberta in *Alberta v. Nilsson* (2002, par. 62)

Unlike expropriation, where traditional, well-established common law principles demand compensation (negated only by a clear statutory statement to the contrary), *regulatory* changes that affect property and which result in a practical loss of use rarely result in compensation. Here are six examples to consider.

Example #1: A three-decade regulatory freeze in Alberta

In the late 1950s, Bill Nilsson, then a young farmer, bought 160 acres near Edmonton and operated a farm and cattle auction business on it for the next decade-and-a-half. In 1976, Nilsson applied to the Ministry of the Environment in order to obtain permission to build a mobile home park on part of his property. Permission was necessary due to a 1974 decision by the province to create the North Edmonton Restricted Development Area (RDA), a designation that, as the name implies, restricted development without permission from the Province. In response to his application, the government of Alberta refused permission, and publicly asserted the land was to be preserved for use as a greenbelt or parkland at some future date (*Alberta (Minister of Infrastructure) v. Nilsson*, 2002).

Given that Nilsson could not develop that section of his property, he considered selling it to the government. However, the province's tender was for only $2,500 an acre, compared to a government purchase price of $10,000 per acre for land on either side of his property. Nilsson refused.

Negotiations continued and during the recession in the early 1980s Nilsson agreed to sell at the offered price on condition he could retain the right to appeal to the Land Compensation Board. That same board later awarded him $15,000 per acre. Rather than accept the board's award to Nilsson, the provincial government refused and went to court. At the Court of Queen's Bench in 1999, Nilsson won and was awarded $9.1 million in principal and compound interest, as well as costs. However, the government continued to fight until 2003 when the Supreme Court of Canada refused to hear the province's appeal (*Alberta v. Nilsson*, 2002).

As it happened, the original justification for the Restricted Development Area and the subsequent denial of the proposed trailer park development—a greenbelt designation—was never true. In reality, the provincial government wanted the land for an eventual ring road and utility corridor (*Alberta v. Nilsson*, 2002: 25). That fact, along with civil servant misgivings about the publicly offered reasons and cabinet discussions which admitted that full compensation should have been given, did not surface until evidence was introduced in court. Those facts were affirmed by the Justice in the Court of Queen's Bench trial and again by the appeals court judge in 1999:

> I am mindful of the heavy onus that Nilsson bears in this case to establish the serious tort of abuse of public office. I appreciate the distinction between a negligent tort and an intentional tort. I also appreciate that a finding that the cabinet committed this intentional tort requires a finding of dishonest or bad faith conduct. However, I am persuaded on the evidence that employing the R.D.A. regulation under the Act as then written to freeze land for eventual use as a transportation and utility corridor does show dishonesty and bad faith. (Referenced in *Alberta v. Nilsson*, 2002: 105)

That the government designated the land as a greenbelt or possible park and not as a possible highway and utility corridor was straightforward, albeit deceitful; it did so to avoid triggering two provincial statutes, the

Public Highways Development Act and the Public Works Act. Both required full compensation. A designation of green space or parkland—a regulatory taking—did not.

Thus, for 29 years, the province of Alberta, by regulation and by constant appeals of lower court decisions, forced the farmer to take his struggle for full and just compensation all the way to the Supreme Court of Canada. It is almost unnecessary to note that few people can afford to battle a provincial government for three decades and all the way to Canada's highest court. Moreover, had Nilsson been injured during that time or faced financial difficulty, he may well have been forced to cease his efforts, and the government of Alberta would have "won" through dishonest means.

This example clearly demonstrates the problem with regulatory takings: public authorities can, without the niceties of expropriation and without incurring liability to compensate as a matter of common law and of the Expropriation Act, confine the land's uses to their own purposes. In doing so, they achieve the effects of an expropriation but save the cost. In this case, it is useful to note that had the province of Alberta in fact wanted Nilsson's land for its stated purpose—a greenbelt or parkland—Nilsson would not have been eligible for full compensation for the government-imposed regulatory loss. The Nilsson case points to the clear need for regulatory actions to be converted to "akin to expropriation" actions in order to give property owners just compensation.

Example #2: How regulation made Coquitlam private property "sterile"

In 2005, the city of Coquitlam, British Columbia, widened a local road, which caused the nearby creek to encroach upon a privately-owned 1.5 acre parcel of land. Also, an environmental company hired by the city declared a seepage ditch in the centre of the property (and which contained only mud and not flowing water), to be a fish habitat. This designation meant the land was, in addition to being subject to municipal regulation, also subject to provincial and federal jurisdiction—this despite the fact, as the owner noted, the ditch was a mere trickle and could never support fish (*Victoria Times Colonist*, 2006: A4).

Barry and Linda Sheridan had owned the property for 18 years and planned to subdivide it into ten building lots, the proceeds from which would fund their retirement. The 1.5 acre parcel had originally been touched only at one corner by the creek. However, the declaration of their land as a "fish habitat," combined with the now-increased 24-metre setbacks because of the diversion on the corner of the property, led the city to declare the entire 1.5 acre parcel "sterile." That designation meant no development could take place, and the land was thus worth little in practical terms. The city of Coquitlam offered compensation, $38,000 (*Tri-City News*, 2005: 1), but only for the portion of the land altered by the stream. (No compensation was offered for the rest of the property declared sterile.)[1] The city's assessed value for that same land the year before it was declared sterile was $449,000 and the Sheridans paid taxes on that same assessment (O'Neill, 2005).

That Coquitlam could declare the Sheridans' land sterile results from the federal Fisheries Act, which declares that "No person shall carry on any work or undertaking that results in the harmful alteration, disruption or destruction of fish habitat" (Canada, 2011: Sec 35 (1)). The law is a reasonable attempt to safeguard fish stocks, but in the case of the Sheridans, it meant that land was, by fiat and subsequent regulation, initially unavailable for use and devalued without any compensation offered.

The Sheridans were eventually successful in convincing the city to re-zone their property for a ten-lot housing development (by 2007). However, the re-zoning only occurred after the Sheridans hired their own Qualified Environmental Professional to analyze the land in question, and at a substantial cost to themselves (Barry Sheridan, interview with author on October 24, 2011 and November 1, 2011).

The relevant question for this book is what if the city of Coquitlam had never approved the re-zoning? The Sheridan case is an example of where a new regulatory designation significantly reduces the value of a property, and where the local municipality never offered full compensation. The initial regulatory taking was akin to a government arbitrarily reaching into an individual's RRSP account, cashing in some stocks, and removing a portion of that money from the account.

---

1   Several European countries (including Germany, the Netherlands, Poland, and Sweden) as well as Israel compensate for such partial regulatory takings. Austria, Finland, the United States, France, and the United Kingdom also provide some measure of compensation in such instances, though it is more limited. See Alterman, 2010 and the discussion later in this paper on comparisons of international takings.

Example #3: Regulatory freezing: CPR, Vancouver, and the Arbutus Corridor

In 1886, British Columbia granted the Canadian Pacific Railway (CPR) land in the city of Vancouver for the construction of a railway line. During the course of the twentieth century, rail usage of the line decreased and by 1999, the company formally began the process of discontinuing rail operations on the corridor, now known as the "Arbutus Corridor." Soon thereafter, the CPR put forward proposals to develop the property for residential and commercial purposes. At that point, in 2000, the city of Vancouver passed a bylaw to declare the corridor, 22 kilometres long, as a public thoroughfare for transportation, including rail, and a "greenway" including public walks, nature trails, and cycle paths (*CPR v. Vancouver* (2006): par. 7).

This bylaw designation was passed under the city's Official Development Plan, or "ODP." Its regulatory authority stems from the *Vancouver Charter*, an act of the Legislature of British Columbia akin to a "municipal act" but specific to the city of Vancouver. Under section 561 of the charter, once development plans are adopted as "official" by the city, they preclude development plans to the contrary. Thus, as the Supreme Court wrote in 2006 (and as all the parties agreed), "The effect of the bylaw was to freeze the redevelopment potential of the corridor and to confine CPR to uneconomic uses of the land" (*CPR v. Vancouver* (2006): par. 8).

The city made it clear that it would not purchase the land and no compensation was offered. In court, the CPR argued it was "intolerable" for the city to seek to keep the land intact without purchasing it (*CPR v. Vancouver* (2006): pars. 4-5). The CPR argued, first, that the effect of the bylaw was to freeze the redevelopment potential of the corridor and to confine the CPR to uneconomic uses of the land, which it argued was unfair and unreasonable; second, the CPR also asserted that the bylaw was *ultra vires* (outside of the powers) of the city and should be struck down; third, that the bylaw suffered from procedural irregularities and should also be struck down on that account, and the combination of the foregoing meant that the CPR was owed compensation (*CPR v. Vancouver* (2006): par. 8).

The Supreme Court of Canada disagreed with all three assertions. In 2006, the high court ruled the bylaw was not outside the powers of the city (par 21), and that just because the city regulated the land to be a public thoroughfare, that action did not make it akin to a street (which would have required compensation). Writing for the majority, Chief Justice Beverley McLachlin offered this reasoning:

> I cannot accept this argument. Stipulating that a piece of land can be used only as a public thoroughfare in an ODP does not make it a street. It merely freezes the use of the land with a view to preserving it for future development by precluding present uses that might interfere with that development. In this case, for example, residential and commercial development cannot take place on the corridor because that might interfere with it being developed in the future for purposes of public passage. For the time being, however, the corridor remains private land in the hands of CPR. (*CPR v. Vancouver* (2006): par. 23)

The Chief Justice also made this observation:

> Finally, CPR argues that the bylaw is invalid because its effect is not to designate land but to regulate it. Regulation, it argues, is not appropriate for an ODP. Again, there is no merit in this argument. The bylaw does not regulate the use of land, but merely designates the corridor for use as a public thoroughfare (par. 25). Its real complaint is that the bylaw prevents it from developing or using the corridor for economically profitable purposes. This amounts, it argues, to a *de facto* taking of its land, requiring compensation. (par. 27 and 28)

In reaching her conclusion—that "freezing" was not equivalent to *de facto* expropriation (a regulatory taking in this book)—the Court pointed to common law precedent:

> CPR argues that at common law, a government act that deprives a landowner of all reasonable use of its land constitutes a *de facto* taking and imposes an obligation on the government to compensate the landowner. For a *de facto* taking requiring compensation at common law, two requirements must be met: (1) an acquisition of a beneficial

interest in the property or flowing from it, and (2) removal of all reasonable uses of the property. In my view, neither requirement of this test is made out here. (par. 30 and 31)[2]

In ruling against the CPR's claim for compensation, Chief Justice McLachlin reasoned that CPR did not succeed in showing that the city acquired a beneficial interest in the land. "The city has gained nothing more than some assurance that the land will be used or developed in accordance with its vision, without even precluding the historical or current use of the land. This is not the sort of benefit that can be construed as a "tak[ing]", wrote McLachlin (par. 33). She also asserted that the "bylaw does not remove all reasonable uses of the property." Chief Justice McLachlin also argued the bylaw did not prevent "the CPR from using its land to operate a railway, the only use to which the land has ever been put during the history of the City" (par. 34). Lastly, she asserted "the bylaw acknowledges the special nature of the land as the only such intact corridor existing in Vancouver, and expands upon the only use the land has known in recent history" (par. 34).

On the question of similarity to expropriation, McLachlin resorted to a technical reason, noting that expropriation under provincial legislation requires an actual "taking of land by an expropriating authority under an enactment without the consent of the owner" (par. 35). Thus, reasoned McLachlin, "Since by statute there is no taking or expropriation here, there is no inconsistency with the Expropriation Act and s. 2(1) [the passage of the Act that discusses expropriation compensation] compensation cannot apply" (par. 36) for the Court.

An analysis

On the judgment itself, first, it was unclear what "reasonable uses" the CPR could have for the land when it was prevented from developing it for a use other than a public pathway. In the same vein, conversely, the Crown did obtain a "beneficial interest" inasmuch as the land's uses would be confined to the city's own preferences, thereby conferring upon it a benefit.

---

2   The Court cited *Mariner Real Estate Ltd. v. Nova Scotia* (Attorney General) (1999), 177 D.L.R. (4th) 696 (N.S.C.A.), at p. 716; *Manitoba Fisheries Ltd. v. The Queen*, [1979] 1 S.C.R. 101; and *The Queen in Right of British Columbia v. Tener*, [1985] 1 S.C.R. 533.

While the original bylaw in 2000 allowed for rail, the reality was that after having already abandoned the line for that purpose in the latter part of the 20th century, the CPR was not likely to restart a rail line in the middle of a densely populated urban neighbourhood. In fact, the railway had actually been decommissioned under the *National Transportation Act*. Had this point about the subsisting possibility of use as a rail line been advanced, it might well have been dismissed as disingenuous. As it was, all the parties in court agreed that the local bylaw in this instance froze all uses. Moreover, given that the bylaw also proscribed a SkyTrain line on the land (the type of light rail used in Vancouver and its environs) it was clear that the city's intended effect was to ensure the land was used exclusively for purposes akin to that of a public park or pedestrian walkway: for pedestrians and cyclists, not for large-scale automated private or public transportation. Insofar as the CPR was restricted to only historic uses of the land (a railway), it was akin to arguing that someone with a private pond that once contained fish, could only ever use it to drop a fishing line in, but could never swim, paddle, or boat upon it.

Second, "*reasonable uses*" was defined by the city, which the Court clearly acknowledges when it wrote that "residential and commercial development cannot take place on the corridor because that might interfere with it being developed in the future for purposes of public passage (par. 25, emphasis added). Thus, any use of the property beyond re-starting a railway line is tightly linked to the priorities of the regulator, the city.

Third, while the Court was on solid technical grounds when it argued that the Expropriation Act did not apply, and that the *Vancouver Charter* expressly obviated any notion that regulated property could be considered "taken" and thus eligible for compensation, the Court's reasoning, following that of the city, was circular: A bylaw exists based upon provincial legislation and which allows for regulation to freeze property; the bylaw defines such freezing as incomparable to expropriation; therefore the proof that no regulatory act is akin to expropriation in is in the bylaw—which already defines such a comparison as invalid.

The analysis skirted the straightforward question: given that the company possessed the land for over a century, and regardless of whether the intended development was to the liking of the city, did the city's freeze constitute a highly restrictive denial of CPR's ability to use the land in any way it wished? The answer was clearly "yes."

Fourth, the Supreme Court's judgment ignored a common sense case for compensation, even for land still deemed "private." To recap the example given in *Belfast Corporation v. O.D. Cars Ltd.* (1960), while the House of Lords did not grant compensation in response to a denied development permit, *Lord Radcliffe did note that when compensation was provided, it was "on the basis that property, itself retained, had been injuriously affected"* (emphasis added) (*Belfast Corporation v. O.D. Cars Ltd.*, supra, at 523). In other words, while unwilling to equate regulatory restrictions with actual expropriation, Lord Radcliffe yet recognized that compensation was, on occasion, deserving—not on the basis of an exact similarity to expropriation, which the House of Lords did not accept, "but on the basis that property, itself retained, had been injuriously affected"—which it did.

Even in *Alberta v. Nilsson* (2002), while deciding lower courts were correct in ruling against the notion that the regulations themselves were akin to expropriation (but while awarding compensation on other grounds) the Court of Appeal of Alberta yet found it necessary to leave the door open for the possibility that regulation could, in some circumstance at some future point, be akin to expropriation: "We do not exclude the possibility that in an exceptional case the nature or extent of restrictions imposed on land use might be so significant that a *de facto* taking of the property has occurred," wrote the Court (par. 62).

McLachlin's reasoning on the technical nature of the *Vancouver Charter* was correct. However, other aspects of the ruling were a departure from precedent. While citing *Mariner Resources*, where Cromwell J.A. (now Cromwell J. of the Supreme Court of Canada) also required that the plaintiff show acquisition of a beneficial interest, other cases yet existed, including some appellate ones, that did not require beneficial interest; yet the Supreme Court of Canada proceeded as if they did not exist. Professor Russell Brown notes just this and lists several past judgments where regulatory takings were seen as akin to the consequences of expropriation without compensation:

In *Casamiro Resource Corp. v. British Columbia* (Attorney General), British Columbia was alleged to have constructively taken 19 mineral claims when it reclassified a park in which the mineral claims were situated. At trial, MacKinnon J. found that, because the reclassification precluded the issuance of resource permits within park boundaries, a constructive taking had been effected. "The fact," he added, "that the province does not gain the mineral rights does not alter the situation in any way." Meaning that the question of whether British Columbia actually acquired the mineral rights was irrelevant.

For the Court of Appeal, Southin J.A. affirmed that it would view the withholding of access to mineral claimholders as a constructive taking. Observing that "[t]he diminution of rights does not always amount to a taking which as a matter of law is equivalent to expropriation," she concluded nevertheless that the necessary threshold had been met, "the grants hav[ing] been turned into meaningless pieces of paper." As such, the Crown's regulation of the plaintiff's enjoyment of an interest in land—by which the Crown acquired no equitable or legal interest in that land—was a "taking ... without compensation." (Brown, 2007: 323–324)

In addition, Brown cites *Rock Resources Inc. v. British Columbia* (2003) and *Alberta v. Nilsson* (2002) as two other examples of appellate pronouncements where the lack of proprietary interest by the public authority was not determinative on the question of whether regulatory takings took place.

In the case of *Rock Resources*, writing for the majority at the British Columbia Court of Appeal, Justice Finch stated that the plaintiff's mineral claims were worth more than "nothing" (quoted in Brown, 2007: 324). Also, notwithstanding the fact there was no tangible gain to the Crown, the Court of Appeal found that a taking of "a property right or interest held by the plaintiff" had been effected (quoted in Brown, 2007: 324-25). Similarly, in *Alberta v. Nilsson*, the Alberta Court of Appeal noted the following:

Expropriation generally involves an absolute transfer of title. However, some cases have held that something less than an absolute taking may amount to *de facto* expropriation. In such cases, while title nominally rested with the original owner, the degree of interference with the owner's property rights mandated compensation for loss of the property. (Quoted in Brown, 2007: 325)

In sum, the Supreme Court of Canada's ruling in *CPR v. Vancouver* broke with precedent; in addition, the judgment was a reminder to property owners that the current state of the law in Canada, and now reinforced by this particular court decision, is that regulatory takings by governments can restrain use to such an extent as to also make property virtually worthless for the property owner. The nonsensical position that the law on regulatory takings is now left with the Supreme Court of Canada ruled in *CPR v. Vancouver* is as follows: (1) regulatory (*de facto*) takings can be the subject of liability, but (2) only where the public authority actually acquires a beneficial interest. In short, the Supreme Court of Canada confused a regulatory taking with a real (expropriation) taking.

Example #4: A general taking—British Columbia's 1973 Agricultural Land Reserve

In 1973, the province of British Columbia introduced the *BC Land Commission Act*, the legal tool that created the province's Agricultural Land Reserve (ALR) between 1974 and 1976. The ALR was created with the justification that in a mountainous province, the small portion of land that could be devoted to farming should be protected. While boundaries have shifted over time (some land has been removed from the reserve and some has been added), the ALR comprises approximately 4.7 million hectares, or about five percent of the province's land mass (British Columbia, undated a).

While that percentage seems small, it is critical to note that most of British Columbia is owned by governments. Ninety-four percent of British Columbia is owned by the provincial government, one percent is owned by the federal Crown Including Indian reserves, Defence lands, federal harbours), and the remainder (5%) is owned privately (British Columbia, undated b). Thus, by placing much of the privately-owned agricultural land in a reserve unavailable for most other uses, the provincial government has taken legal and equitable control over the use and value of much of the remaining portion of land it doesn't already own.

Whatever one thinks of the justification for the land reserve, the regulation and restriction on land use and compensation for the same are two distinct matters. There are indeed valid reasons to regulate or restrict how some land is used by its owner; few people would think a new hog operation in the middle of a suburb is a desirable "neighbour." However, the BC restriction on land use has had at least two unintended, though not unanticipated consequences.

First, the restriction tightened the supply of land available for housing development. That squeezed supply. The result is higher-than-necessary prices for housing in a province that most years has strong in-migration. That is especially harmful to the poor and to renters, who must devote a greater share of their income to accommodation than otherwise necessary.

The second is that while property values in nominal terms have risen in BC over the last four decades, ALR-designated land has risen less rapidly. That is of no small consequence in relative terms given that the cost of other property, which a present-day owner of agricultural-designated land might wish to buy one day for retirement, has risen even faster (Campbell, 2006: 11–12). The loss of use has directly affected value.

Example #5: Ontario's wide green swath—minus compensation

In February 2005, the government of Ontario announced a "greenbelt" around Greater Toronto (created by an Order-in Council in February that year but retroactive to December 16, 2004) (Ontario, 2005a). The greenbelt's purpose was three-fold: to "protect against the loss and fragmentation of the agricultural land base and [to support] agriculture as the predominant land use"; to permanently protect "the natural heritage and water resource systems that sustain ecological and human health"; and to "provide for a diverse range of economic and social activities associated with rural communities, agriculture, tourism, recreation and resource uses" (Ontario, 2005b: 4). The provincial government's general justification was that by protecting 1.8 million acres of sensitive land from development, "the greenbelt protects the water we drink and the air we breathe" (Ontario, 2008b).

The functional aspects of the Greenbelt Plan were statutorily created through 2006 amendments made to the province's *Planning and Conservation Land Statute Law Amendment Act* (Ontario, 2011a: 1). The changes directed municipalities to ensure that through the use of official plans, zoning bylaws, and site plan control, all Ontario municipal decisions made under the act would be required to conform to the Greenbelt Plan.

The Greenbelt Plan allowed existing uses in effect prior to the plan's implementation to continue (Ontario, 2005b: 38). However, restrictions on future use made it clear "where major urban growth cannot take place" and that "Reductions or deletions to the Greenbelt area will not be considered" (Ontario, 2008b: 1). (On the other hand, expansions were welcome if a local municipality or other organization made such a request (Ontario, 2011b: 4 and 6)). As the Ontario government notes, development within the greenbelt is severely restricted: "The Greenbelt Plan permits intensification, including infill development, in existing settlement areas" (Ontario, 2011a: 4).

In short, land is frozen and available for prior usage only. However, even then, as the next example illustrates, even that prior designation cannot stand if the provincial government or a local municipality decides a new designation applies, one that further restricts use.

Example #6: Ontario's wetlands designations

The province of Ontario has a program to designate marshes, bogs, swamps, and fens (wetlands that accumulate peat) as "provincially significant wetlands." Designations are based on a points system which includes a biological, social, hydrological, and "special features" components (Ontario, 2008a: 1–4). Under the *Conservation Authorities Act*, local municipalities must comply with the act. The combination of good intentions, the provincial act, and required local zoning obviously intends to restrict use. However, those restrictions can have unintended though not unanticipated consequences for the use and value of such real property and, also of no small importance, unintended consequences for the destruction of selected natural habitats.

Also, even "basic wetland" (not initially considered provincially significant) can later be affected through a regulations permit process called "complexing," which allows basic wetland to be designated Provincially Significant if it is within 750 metres of an existing Provincially Significant Wetland (Ontario, 2008a: 4). This might effectively strip all, and not just some, uses from the property.

In one example from Ottawa, Tony Walker, head of the Goulbourn Landowners Group, describes the results for local property owners of provincial wetlands designation with subsequent city zoning:

> In Ottawa, in 2004, the Ministry of Natural Resources (MNR) and the City of Ottawa initiated a study "to identify wetlands and determine their potential to complex with the Goulbourn Wetland Complex." A letter was sent to the affected landowners indicating a study was

underway and requesting permission to come onto their properties to evaluate their wetland status. The letter did not discuss the process, warn of the potential for designation as a Provincially Significant Wetland, or of the effects on property value ...

The city then used aerial photographs from 2002 to identify potential wetlands. In September 2004, the city's biologist flew over the target properties to identify wetland plants and supplemented this with roadside surveys. In February 2005, the city sent the completed study to MNR, which designated the wetland areas as Provincially Significant Wetland based on their proximity to the existing Goulbourn Wetland Complex and the complexing regulations.

Altogether 262 hectares (about 650 acres) were designated [as Provincially Significant Wetlands] ... In April 2005, the City of Ottawa informed the landowners... of the city's intent to update its official plan to re-zone the affected properties as Provincially Significant Wetlands. This was an information meeting; landowners were permitted to ask questions but their input was not required or requested. The city outlined the history and their ongoing plans to re-zone the affected properties. At no point in the process do the landowners have an opportunity to have their concerns addressed or to object to what is taking place. The landowners can only appeal the Official Plan Amendment to the Ontario Municipal Board (OMB) at their own substantial expense, but this will not affect the provincial designation.

There is also a buffer zone of up to 120 metres around all designated wetlands, where land use is severely restricted. Affected landowners were not informed that they are in the buffer zone, or of the restrictions on their property. The city has stated that it does not intend to compensate landowners for the devaluation of their properties. The effect of these designations is to devalue and freeze private property. (Walker, undated)

In the case of Walker's land specifically, in 2005, the effect of restricted use had a knock-off effect on the value of the land. Walker noted at then market prices, his 20-hectare plot was worth about $125,000. However, with a wetland designation, the price would be less than $20,000, an 84% reduction in his land value (Canada, 2005). Also, and presumably, the effect of such designation for smaller lots would be to completely strip all uses from them.

CHAPTER THREE

The case for compensation for regulatory takings

"Any person who is compelled to surrender property by means of compulsory purchase or other such disposition shall be guaranteed compensation for his loss. Such compensation shall also be guaranteed to any person whose use of land or buildings is restricted by the public administration in such a way that ongoing land use in the affected part of the property is substantially impaired or injury results which is significant in relation to the value of that part of the property concerned."

—Thomas Kalbro on Sweden's approach to compensation for regulatory takings, in Alterman's *Takings International* (2010: 294)

Conservation is not the problem, just the lack of compensation

It is no startling observation to note that people like green space and that few prefer to live near industrial zones or polluted land. It is why land values near a public park such as New York City's Central Park or Vancouver's Stanley Park are more desirable and thus more expensive than those located even in similarly built-up areas within the same cities. Likewise, in terms of nature and wild space, most reasonable people would likely desire that flora and fauna be reasonably protected, especially where legitimate concerns exist over extinction.

The existence of laws and regulations to such ends are an implicit demonstration of such widespread public sentiment without which such laws and policies would not exist in their current form. The desires may be reasonable and laudable, or unreasonable and ill-advised, depending on specific examples. The key issue for policymakers is the lack of compensation for property owners where a new regulation, land claim, bylaw, heritage designation, federal endangered species designation, or other government action, reduces the use of their property (and often with a concurrent reduction of value of their assets) and/or impedes their ability to make a living. Insofar as a public agency restricts the use of property, compensation is due. The cost of some popular "public" preference for private property, even where warranted, ought not to be borne by the property owner, but by the public at large.

To cite the Ontario example, the intent of the greenbelt and of wetlands designation—to protect farmland, green space, and significant and sensitive wetlands—is appealing. Most people would like to see nature, to have it protected, and prefer to be near to it. The goal, similar to the creation of a national parks system in the late 19th century, has understandable appeal. However, the creation of a national parks system on Crown land is unlike the problem for property owners that arises in the means of achieving an end for public purposes. In Ontario, the provincial government offered no compensation for the 1.8 million acres of private land that it declared off limits to development.

The cost of green space and other public goods should not fall on the property owner any more than the burden of paying for a local road improvement used by all should be assigned to one homeowner in a neighbourhood of 20 houses. Or consider the entirely reasonable proposition put forward on who should pay for pollution: polluters, and not the general public. In support of pollution control measures, environmentalists argue, quite properly, that polluters should be forced to "internalize" the externalities flowing from their activities. Similarly, it is entirely reasonable to force society to internalize the cost of a new regulation that significantly reduces the use of private property, rather than have the property owner bear the cost of a public regulation that would impose the publicly-chosen externality on a few.

That would serve two purposes: First, it would make conservation less an "us versus them" debate. Instead, the issue would then be about the proper compensation for conservation and the desirability of the latter. Second, and concurrently, requiring compensation would enable the public and governments to accurately assess the true cost of a desired regulation as it is applied to private property. In that sense, it would place regulatory takings on the same level as expropriation takings. However, for those who favour the greenbelt and see it as only an environmental and lifestyle issue and not also a property rights issue, the question of compensation is barely considered.

For example, in a 2008 report from the Friends of the Greenbelt Foundation, the report's policy recommendations include the promotion of such green areas, including: centralizing authority over such areas, subsidies for farmers and "buy local" proponents, and school programs that praise the Greenbelt (Carter-Whitney, 2008: 4–8). The report also recommends that students not be allowed to graduate from high school unless they "obtain a food knowledge certificate" (74).

The closest the report comes to suggesting anything resembling compensation is when it urges governments to subsidize farmers: "It is also beneficial to make long-term public funding available to recognize and support the landscape conservation work that farmers undertake on behalf of the public," writes the author (69). But the context of the paragraph is not property rights; it is about building support for a regional farm economy, not about compensation for loss of property. In another section, the report advocates compensation, but again, not for lost value, just for farmers that implement some environmental stewardship measures (72).

Still, despite those and other recommendations, nowhere in the 95-page report is the issue of compensation for restricted use (regulatory takings) mentioned. Instead, the report uses good versus evil Manichean language (it refers to "foes" on page 41). This is unhelpful. Instead, such authors and others should conceive of the possibility that conservation is compatible with property rights so long as compensation is part of the larger, more holistic approach to green space development.

There is a clear case for compensation for regulatory takings; three reasons stand out.

1. There is an obvious loss of use and value because of regulatory takings

As with the Friends of the Greenbelt Foundation document, a 37-page, 2006 report from the David Suzuki Foundation on BC's Agricultural Land Reserve (ALR) makes no mention of the need to compensate property owners for land frozen for agricultural use only. As with the Ontario report, the Suzuki foundation urges some subsidies for farmers, but does not recognize the devalued properties or compensation for the same.

However, the Suzuki Foundation implicitly acknowledges the case for compensation when it outlines the dramatic difference between the value of parcels of land inside and outside of the province's land reserve, as when it cites the pressure to develop land near urban areas. The Foundation notes:

> Good farmland in parcels of 20 hectares or more in the Fraser Valley costs between $50,000 and $100,000 per hectare. Add the permitted house to a small parcel and the value can escalate enormously. Soaring urban housing costs are increasing the upward pressure… The disparity in land values escalates even further when other uses come into play. Turn a hectare of farmland into an industrial park and the land can be worth $1 million. One estimate valued 55 hectares of land that may be excluded [from the ALR] near the centre of Richmond for public infrastructure and commercial development at more than $6 million per hectare. (Campbell, 2006: 11–12)

2. Foreign companies are treated better than domestic property owners

A new argument for compensation based on regulatory takings is emerging as a result of Canada's participation in NAFTA. As Russell Brown summarizes it: "Under Article 1110 of NAFTA, an 'investor' from the United States or Mexico who has an 'investment' in Canada may initiate a claim to determine through international arbitration whether Canada has imposed a 'measure' that is 'tantamount to… expropriation, thereby triggering a right in the investor to compensation'" (Brown, 2007: 335–336).

Indeed, Article 201 defines a "measure" as "any law, regulation, procedure, requirement or practice" (NAFTA, undated: Article 201). Article 1139 is broad in its definition of an investment for which a claim of injury may be made under the agreement. It includes: an enterprise; an equity security of an enterprise; a debt security of an enterprise; an interest in an enterprise that entitles the owner to share in income or profits of the enterprise (including on dissolution); real estate or other property, tangible or intangible, acquired in the expectation or used for the purpose of economic benefit or other business purposes; and interests arising from the commitment of capital or other resources in the territory of a Party to economic activity in such territory (NAFTA, undated: Article 1139).

Brown notes that two tribunals have required that a measure be tantamount to expropriation if expropriation clauses are to be triggered.[1] However, he also notes another NAFTA tribunal ruling, *Metalclad Corporation v. United Mexican States*, where the American company (Metalclad) was entitled to compensation after a municipal construction permit was denied by a Mexican state governor on ecological grounds (Brown, 2007: 337), this under section 1110. The tribunal awarded compensation for acquisition and construction costs and stated that,

> expropriation under NAFTA includes not only open, deliberate and acknowledged takings of property, such as outright seizure or formal or obligatory transfer of title in favour of the host State, but also covert or incidental interference with the use of property which has the effect of depriving the owner, in whole or in significant part, of the use or reasonably-to-be-expected economic benefit of property even if not necessarily to the obvious benefit of the host State. (*Metalclad Corporation v. The United Mexican States*, 2000: par. 103)

Thus, given the scope of the assets for which compensation may be claimed (note Article 201 included "regulation" as one measure which may be actionable), it appears, as Brown notes, to raise the question of whether NAFTA investors outside of Canada have superior protection from regulatory takings over those who reside within Canada (Brown, 2007: 336). The protection afforded foreign companies under NAFTA is not odious or undesirable; the very point of free trade agreements is to provide for free trade between signatories to such treaties. It is only the dichotomy between the compensation a domestic individual or company would receive in the event of a regulatory taking (nil if *CPR v. Vancouver* is an indication) and that which a foreign investor in Canada would receive (at least some compensation, if *Metalclad Corporation v. The United Mexican States* is an indication).

Also of note, the same argument applies to all offshore investors from counterpart states under the dozens of free trade agreements and Foreign Investment Promotion and Protection agreements (FIPAs) into which

---

1   *S.D. Myers Inc. v. Canada*, [2002] 121 I.L.R. 73 (UNCITRAL Panel) [S.D. Myers]; *Pope and Talbot Inc. v. Canada*, [2002] 122 I.L.R. 203 (Arb. Trib.) [Pope and Talbot].

Canada has entered (Foreign Affairs and International Trade, 2012).[2] As Brown points out, "all FIPAs to which Canada is a party effectively preclude the parties' ability to take except where the taking is for a public purpose, effected under due process of law, non-discriminatory and compensated" (Brown, 2011: 4-56).

3. Even the Swedes and Dutch compensate—Canada fares poorly in international compensation comparisons

Canada's non-compensation for regulatory takings sets it apart from other major Western countries. In a survey of 13 nations, Canada and Australia are the most restrictive about compensating for regulatory takings. As Rachelle Alterman writes in her introduction to the survey (and from which I will draw heavily in this section), "Among the 13 countries, Canada ranks as offering the lowest degree of compensation rights" (2010: 3).

To delve into the details, Alterman and the other authors divide regulatory takings into three types: major takings, direct partial takings, and indirect partial takings.

Major takings or "major injuries" are defined by Alterman et al. as a situation where regulation extinguishes all or nearly all of a property's value. She notes that all 13 countries surveyed address this taking in some manner, albeit with different language: "categorical" or "per se" taking in the United States and "constructive expropriation" or "de facto taking" in Canada (Alterman, 2010: 23-24).

Direct partial takings are caused by regulatory decisions that apply to some plot of land that suffers the depreciation—"the usual conception of a regulatory taking," writes Alterman (2010: 24).

Indirect partial takings refer to injuries that may be caused by regulatory decisions that apply to other plots of land in the vicinity (the precise geographic definition varies by country) (Alterman, 2012: 24).

---

2   At present, Canada has free trade agreements with the United States, Mexico, Honduras, Panama, Jordan, Colombia, Peru, Costa, Rica, Chile, Israel, and with the European Free Trade Association. FIPAs are in effect with 27 countries, negotiations have concluded with two others, and 14 others are in negotiation.

Canada fares poorly in all three categories. On major takings, under Canadian law, "a landowner generally must show that there has been a removal of all reasonable uses of the property; case law has not recognized anything less," writes Alterman (2010: 37). Indeed, as noted in *CPR v. Vancouver* (2006), the Supreme Court of Canada ruled that a claimant must also prove there has been an acquisition of a beneficial interest in the property to claim a regulatory taking has occurred that is akin to expropriation (par. 30 and 31).

In contrast, Poland, Germany, Sweden, Israel, and the Netherlands all provide the broadest compensation rights for major regulatory takings. Unsurprisingly, given the weak and narrow compensation rights available for property owners in Canada in the case of *major* takings, those who suffer from partial takings (direct or indirect) are not compensated at all. That Canadian practice stands in contrast to most other countries surveyed (table 1). In fact, compared with Canada, the European Union has relatively strong property rights protection, so much so that some member countries (Sweden is a notorious example cited by Alterman) have been forced to change their laws to comply with the European Union's property protection clause in the European Convention (Carss-Fisk, 2001: 5). It is why Alterman comments that, "Had Canada been in Europe, some aspects of its law on major takings may not have survived ECHR [European Commission on Human Rights] scrutiny" (2010: 37).

Summary—the "winner takes all" problem

Problematically for property owners in Canada (domestic ones at least), the current state of policy inertia in Canada as regards regulatory takings leads to a "winner takes all" approach where governments can "freeze" partial or whole parcels of land. This occurs where governments are in the legal wrong (as in *Nilsson v. Alberta* (1999)) where a regulatory designation, albeit a deceitful one, was used in the interim to avoid proper and existing expropriation compensation. This also occurs where governments are in the legal "right" (as in *CPR. v. Vancouver*). In addition, the Supreme Court of Canada affirmation in the latter case does not remove the real-world effect of private land frozen for public purposes and without compensation—or without proper compensation. It only puts the problem of regulatory takings, the lack of compensation, and the lack of property rights in legal concrete. To break that concrete apart will require legislative reform, the parameters of which are discussed next.

Table 1: Compensation for regulatory takings?

Major takings	Direct partial takings	Indirect partial takings
Canada		
Minimal, highly restrictive, rare	NO	NO
Australia		
Minimal, highly restrictive, rare	NO	NO
Austria		
Broader but ambiguous	Occasionally	NO
Finland		
Broader but ambiguous	Occasionally	Broad compensation rights
France		
Minimal but broader than Canada	Rarely	NO
Germany		
Broadest compensation rights	YES	For public infrastructure harm
Greece		
Minimal and restrictive	Rarely	NO
Israel		
Broadest compensation rights	YES	Broadest compensation rights
Netherlands		
Broadest compensation rights	YES	Broadest compensation rights
Poland		
Broadest compensation rights	YES	Selected cases but inconsistent
Sweden		
Broadest compensation rights	YES	Public infrastructure and environmental regulation harm
United Kingdom		
Minimal but broader than Canada	Rarely	Rarely
United States		
Broader but ambiguous	Occasionally	NO

Source: Alterman, 2010.

CHAPTER FOUR

The "most devilishly difficult question"—when to compensate for regulatory takings

"German planning law provides clear answers to almost every conceivable situation where an injury to property values may arise. The law does grant compensation rights, including for partial takings of any magnitude, but there is a time limit. The balance struck is widely accepted."
—Rachelle Alterman in *Takings International* (2010: 271)

In his 2005 article, "One Step Beyond Nozick's Minimal State: The Role of Forced Exchanges in Political Theory," University of Chicago law professor Richard Epstein notes that "deciding which forms of regulation are permissible without compensation and which are not presents some of the most devilishly difficult questions that arise in the operation of any mature legal system" (2005: 291). Obviously, the devil is in the details and Epstein points out that even Locke, the father of property theory, justified the removal of resources from the commons by noting we would all starve if we had to wait for uniform consent to act, "which was his way of noting that the coordination problem from unanimous consent was intractable" (2005: 297).

The point here is not about the commons, but rather when governments are justified in their regulatory actions (or in expropriation actions, though not discussed in this book). Epstein, who is sympathetic to calls for a more limited role for governments, nevertheless disagrees with Nozick's belief that a state can come into being voluntarily—"[Nozick's] argument loses all its zip once it is recognized that forced exchanges are built into foundations of any organized society," writes Epstein, who continues,

They [forced exchanges] are first built in the definition of property and liberty and their correlative duties, and next in the creation of a single sovereign with monopoly power over all individuals within its territory. If however, the method of forced exchanges is needed to explain and justify the creation of a principle state, there is no reason why the same methodology cannot be used to explain commonplace institutions that are developed once that state is established. Quite simply, the logic of forced exchanges is to allow for Pareto improvements that voluntary transactions cannot achieve (Epstein, 2005: 305).

Pareto improvements—defined as an action that helps at least one person and harms no one—are indeed a useful general guide. Should a legislature wish to protect private property from regulatory takings, there is the preliminary question of whether all regulatory takings will attract compensation and, if not, then at what threshold of restriction the regulatory taking will attract compensation. To get to that end goal, though, will require some specifics.

So let us look first at the principle to be enunciated; second, at the existing high barrier to compensation for regulatory takings; third, what regulatory takings should attract compensation and fourth, how much? To help this process along and provide clarity, examples on what regulatory takings are compensated and at what levels will be offered from Europe and Israel. Readers should also review table 1 in chapter 3 for the existing practice among the 13 countries surveyed by Alterman et al. (2010). How other countries approach this matter may serve as a useful starting point.

First, the principle from 1967 Ontario Law Reform Commission

Let's start with the principle for compensation as already applied in existing examples where governments compensate: expropriation. This principle of compensation for intended loss of property is already well established in law and practice. In its 1967 report, the Ontario Law Reform Commission made clear what was at stake:

From its examination of the development of the Canadian law, the Commission has formed the opinion that some of the difficulties with assessing compensation flow from a failure to appreciate that the true basis for it is not to be found in an imaginary haggling over the price to be paid for land in a deal between two private individuals, nor the negotiation of a normal bargain in the market place, *but in the fulfilment by the state of its obligation to repair the injury caused to particular individuals for the public good,* and to minimize the loss, inconvenience, and disturbance to the life of its citizens to as great an extent as possible. (Quoted in *Toronto Area Transit Operating Authority v. Dell Holdings Ltd.* (1997); emphasis added)

Second, precedents and problems

With that principle in mind, recall that as it concerns regulation as akin to expropriation and as quoted in *CPR v. Vancouver* (2006), for a regulatory taking to trigger compensation at common law it must contain two elements: 1) an acquisition of a beneficial interest in the property or flowing from it, and 2) removal of all reasonable uses of the property. If only one element is present, a regulatory taking or any other action cannot be considered a *de facto* expropriation and thus compensation cannot be triggered.

The two-part test is problematic. As evident from *CPR v. Vancouver* (2006), the city argued it had no beneficial interest in the CPR lands. That protected the city from paying compensation in the event a court found that the other requirement—an extinguishment of all reasonable uses of property—had occurred. In Ontario, the greenbelt is yet another example of a regulatory taking without compensation. In both cases, green spaces (Ontario's greenbelt) and public pathways (Vancouver's Arbutus corridor) may well be desirable. The question is one of proper compensation.

Thus, one reform necessary to properly compensate for regulatory takings is to remove the second part of the existing two-part test ("beneficial interest") as it invites abuse to regulate land without moving to expropriate land.

Third, what regulatory takings should attract compensation?

As noted in table 1, takings can be divided into major takings, direct partial takings, and indirect partial takings. To give clear examples: A major taking would be where a government removes or greatly restricts the use of property (and a great portion of the property) as to make it practically unusable for any other purpose than that desired by the government (as in the case of *CPR v. Vancouver* (2006)). A direct partial taking is a regulation that takes part of the property in question. The Alberta government's action vis-à-vis part of Bill Nilsson's farm in the 1970s is an example. An example of an indirect partial taking could be where a government allows a new airport to be built near a neighbourhood. The residents may still be able to reside there in some fashion, but the noise of the airplanes make it less than desirable and property values subsequently drop. In this latter case, the government has not directly regulated the property in question, but its change in a designation for a neighbouring property has led to an indirect taking. Major takings are examined first followed by the other two types.

Major takings: examples on parameters and compensation amounts from abroad

In this category, I will restrict examples of compensation practices to those countries with the broadest compensation rights:

Germany and Sweden   Property owners can initiate a 'transfer-of-title" claim if regulatory actions are delayed (Alterman, 2010: 45). In Germany, a distinction is made between land designated for private use and that designated for public use. Where the land is designated for public use, 14 categories apply. If the municipality does not act quickly to acquire the land, a landowner may demand that the land be acquired (expropriated). However, the municipality may, if the owner is shown to be receiving economically reasonable income from the property (i.e., the land or chattels continue to produce rental income), deny the demand for the expropriation action, though not indefinitely. Because a regulatory taking is illegal in Germany, there is no time limit on the landowners' right to demand a transfer of title claim (and thus compensation). Sweden is similar but with a time limit (Alterman, 2010: 45).

Poland   A special remedy exists for land designated for public use but not taken (expropriated with compensation) within a reasonable time. In such cases, a landowner can force the government to expropriate—far preferable to waiting for regulatory compensation. In fact, when plots of land were designated for public purposes for 10 to 24 years (depending on the example) and were neither compensated for nor expropriated, the European Commission on Human Rights (ECHR) found Poland in violation of the European Union Convention's property protection clause (Alterman, 2010: 44–45).

Israel and the Netherlands   For unique reasons, the government often designates a plot of land for public purposes in advance of expropriation. That regulatory designation, though, can and does trigger a two-part process for compensation: first, compensation due to the restricted use and accompanying loss of value of the land; and second, compensation for the remaining value once expropriated (Alterman, 2010: 46). Critically, for property owners, what this means is that regulation cannot be used to deny compensation; the regulatory action *itself* triggers compensation.

Compensation for direct partial takings: International examples

Compensation for direct partial takings varies among the 13 countries surveyed by Alterman et al. with the important comment noted that Canada and Australia rarely ever compensate for direct regulatory takings. Alterman et al. (2010) find that:

Finland   Statutory law provides that if an owner of a heritage building cannot produce a reasonable return, the owner is entitled to full compensation from the state or national government (50).

Austria   Four out of nine states in Austria provide for partial takings compensation, including in instances of reduced development rights, restricted development rights, and decreased values (50).

United States   Some states recognize partial takings in law, though the damage to value must be significant, ranging from 60 percent to 85 percent, or even higher. One notable exception is Oregon, where under a 2004 ballot initiative, landowners were granted full compensation rights for any type of land-use-related regulatory decision, including planning, zoning, and environmental regulation decisions. That 2004 ballot initiative was replaced in 2007 by another initiative that restricted compensation claims to land use regulations that concern the development of single-family homes, or restrict farming and forestry practices (50–52, 240). Still, the compensation regime is generous.

Poland   Poland grants compensation in principle for direct partial takings based upon "the first zloty" of depreciation in a property's value. In practice though, claimants must demonstrate that they have transferred (sold) the affected property, and that the sale price was less than it would have been under the previous regulation. The level of compensation is based on appraisal; also, property that has been sold to relatives is excluded from such claims (52–53).

Germany Germany provides for partial takings compensation but imposes a limit of seven years in the case of developments from the time an original plan for development was approved. The reasoning in play is that seven years gives a developer an incentive to in fact carry through and is fair warning that if a proposal is not acted on within that time, no guarantee of re-approval should be assumed (or compensation if denied). Exceptions do exist to the seven-year rule. On compensation, the rules are clear: landowners have the right to compensation for a reduction in property values due to a regulation; to development-related expenses made during the approved development phase; and to full compensation rights for any moratorium applied to a proposed development that extends beyond four years (53–55).

Sweden The laws for compensation are similar to those in Germany. Differences include no minimum compensation thresholds (and are thus akin to Polish practice) and even minimum injuries from partial takings are compensable (55).

Israel and the Netherlands Both countries grant full compensation for partial takings and with either no minimum threshold, or a very low one, depending on the taking in question (57). In the Netherlands, to be eligible for compensation, a property owner need only demonstrate a tiny decline in property values, which originates in the notion expressed in this Dutch planning statute: "insofar as the loss cannot be reasonably expected to be borne by the applicant" (57). Also, the Dutch recognize the loss of business income as a compensable category. However, Dutch property owners are expected to try and minimize the damage to local governments. They must apply for compensation within a reasonable time, and "shadow" planning damages are not eligible (i.e., where a development plan that has been proposed, but not yet passed, decreases property values). Also, since 2005, a small administrative fee has been imposed to ward off small claims (60–61).

Compensation for indirect partial takings:
International examples

Lastly, compensation for indirect claims—e.g., the expansion of a roadway or airport which causes the loss of property use (or decreases the value) is also compensated for in some of the countries surveyed. Canada and Australia do not compensate at all, nor does Austria, France, Greece, or the United States. In contrast:

United Kingdom   The United Kingdom does provide some compensation for partial indirect takings, but only for noise vibration, smell, and artificial lighting (63).

Finland   Finland grants some compensation for landowners indirectly affected by highways and also by environmental regulations (64).

Poland   Polish compensation for indirect regulatory harm is rare (65).

Germany and Sweden   Both countries grant some limited but rare compensation in this instance. In Germany, for example, it is forbidden for new houses to be built by airports (and thus property owners with land near existing or new airports are partly compensated for that restriction). In Sweden, both direct and indirect injuries relating from environmental regulations are compensable, but the depreciation must be of "some significance" (65)

Israel and the Netherlands   Both countries have broad compensation rights for injuries resulting from indirect partial takings. Thresholds are set at 2 percent in the Netherlands. Israel's Knesset has a draft law to abolish most grounds for claims of indirect injuries (66–67).

To grasp how one European country breaks down its various threshold levels and determines the compensation due, see "Table 2: Regulatory compensation in Sweden." It may serve as a useful guide for revisions to Canadian policy on regulatory takings as it offers specific details for a variety of regulatory and land planning areas.

Table 2: Regulatory compensation in Sweden—compensation rights and threshold levels

Type of decision as grounds for compensation	"Qualification threshold" for compensation	Full compensation or deductible threshold
Provisions in a detailed development plan		
Protective provisions for valuable buildings	Current land use is "substantially impaired"—threshold varies	Full compensation
Demolition prohibition for protected buildings	"Significant injury": 15%+	Exceeding the threshold
Order to alter access ways to public areas	None	Full compensation
Change in designated public open space	None	Full compensation
Plan amendment during implementation periods	None	Full compensation
Plan amendment after implementation periods		Full compensation
Refusal to grant a permit		
To replace a building accidentally destroyed	None	Full compensation
To replace a demolished building	"Significant injury": 15%+	Exceeding the threshold
To demolish a building	"Significant injury": 15%+	Exceeding the threshold
Site improvement permit	Current land use is "substantially impaired": 10%+	Full compensation
"Environmental damages" to adjacent properties		
Various planning decisions	"Not a common occurrence": above 2%–5%	Exceeding the threshold

Source: Alterman 2010, 301.

Fourth, how should regulatory takings be calculated?

Example 1: From the Saskatchewan Court of Queen's Bench

In terms of determining compensation, one guideline to reasonableness can be found in Saskatchewan Court of Queen's Bench in *Shamon v. Biggar* [2003] *(Rural Municipality) No. 347*. The guideline concerned expropriation, but can also be applied to regulatory takings. The court offered the following three guidelines to determine fair compensation in a given circumstance, summarized by Alexis Moulton at McLennan Ross (2005). One could look at this as an example of how to compensate a major taking:

1. Determine what a prudent person would pay rather than be ejected from the expropriated lands. In most cases, this will equal the highest and best use of the land expropriated and the value of any improvements thereon. An exception arises where the value assigned to the land expropriated is based on a highest and best use and that, by its nature, contemplates the destruction of an improvement, e.g., trees. In such case, no additional value is to be assigned to lost improvements or consequential damages to the remaining land if a prudent person would have accepted compensation payable based on the expropriated land's highest and best use.

2. Determine what damages the claimant is entitled to for injury caused to the claimant's remaining land, even if the claimant received compensation for the land taken based on its highest and best use. The following further question might be considered: would a prudent person have sold the lands taken for the consideration received and accept the damage resulting to the balance of his or her lands without further compensation?

3. Consider whether the expropriation increased the value of the claimant's remaining lands. (Moulton 2005: 1)

The usefulness of the above guidelines is that both the possible benefit ("increased value") and the possible harm are taken into account. As applied to regulatory compensation, both can and should be applied in the final compensation mix.

Example 2: A guideline from the federal Fisheries Act

Canada rarely compensates for direct regulatory harm (major or direct partial). However, the federal Fisheries Act is a useful example of that rare instance where regulatory costs imposed on property owners (and which constitute "takings") lead governments to admit to the necessity of at least some compensation. For example, sections 20 through 22, which refer to the construction of "fish-ways," allows the federal government, if it deems it necessary for the public interest, to demand a property owner provide an "efficient fish-way or canal," or to require the owner "to pay [for a] complete fish hatchery establishment" that will maintain the annual return of migratory fish (Canada, 2011: Sec. 20 (1) and (2)).

The legislation stipulates that in the event of such a designation, the government "may" pay half of the cost to be incurred by the property owner (Section 21(1)). However, that, of course, still leaves a substantial cost to be incurred by the property owner and raises the question of why full compensation is not also forthcoming. The political answer is that it easier for a government to designate an improvement to a piece of property for public or environmental ends and place the cost (or half the cost) upon the landowner. That is cheaper than expropriation, though in the case of the Fisheries Act, at least some compensation is forthcoming for the regulatory taking. Still, the Fisheries Act at least broaches the possibility of compensation for a new regulatory designation.

Summary on compensation options

As noted, compensation practice and percentages vary widely depending on the type of taking and especially on the jurisdiction. Israel and the Netherlands offer the most compensation (and often in the most cases) compared with the United States, where some property owners (outside of Oregon) are forced to swallow large value losses in the event of a regulatory taking. In Canada, regulatory takings are, with rare exception, never compensated. Based on the preceding, chapter 5 will offer some specific remedies.

CHAPTER FIVE

Detailed recommendations

"Canadian law lacks a robust regulatory takings doctrine."
Bryan P. Schwartz and Melanie P. Bueckert in
Alterman's *Takings International* (2010: 93)

Broad recommendation—treat regulatory takings as akin to expropriation takings

This broad recommendation stems from the example and practice in selected countries that see little or no difference between a loss of use and a loss of value of property, either of which can stem from acts of expropriation or acts of regulation that effect major takings. Germany, Israel, and the Netherlands are models to follow here.

The whole or partial loss of use of property and the often subsequent decline in value of property due to regulation for a public end demands compensation. The principle in play is that where governments wish to use private property for public purposes, the public should bear the cost of that designation, not individual property holders.

Specific recommendations that should be acted upon

Recommendation 1

Canadian governments should follow the example of Germany, Israel, the Netherlands, Poland, and Sweden and fully compensate property owners for major takings (as all five countries do) and direct partial takings (as Israel and the Netherlands do), and to a lesser and limited degree, indirect partial takings.

Rationale

In order to treat regulatory takings as akin to expropriation, major takings and direct partial takings should be compensated as an assumed part of regulatory and planning processes. Indirect partial takings will need to be compensated on more restricted grounds, but should also be considered where use has been restricted by regulations or planning, and property values are harmed as a result.

Recommendation 2

Allow property owners to convert major regulatory takings and direct partial takings into expropriation actions.

Rationale

Where a regulatory or planning action has limited the use of all or portions of a property, federal and provincial law (including municipal law for which provinces are responsible), should allow the property owner to demand title transfer. This would convert a regulatory action into an expropriation action, which would then trigger compensation. This is based on the German and Swedish models for major takings (Alterman, 2010: 45) but is extended here for direct partial takings.

A "common sense" test should apply here: has the new regulation restricted past, existing, or future possible uses in a manner that all or much of the land is "frozen"? If so, the same demand for conversion into an expropriation action should be allowed, and the property owner should be allowed this option after two years from the date of the change in regulation or planning status of the property.

In Canada, had this policy been in effect in the case of Bill Nilsson, the province of Alberta would have been forced to offer significant compensation for his land early on. In the case of *CPR v. Vancouver*, the city of Vancouver would have been required to offer CPR compensation for the Arbutus corridor or expropriate the parcel outright, which would have triggered compensation. Green spaces and other usages are desirable ends and can be described as meeting a public interest test; the critical point is that such takings must be paid for out of the public treasury, given it is the wider public that benefits. For additional clarity, legislation should specify that any attempt to "re-start the clock" by slight changes to the regulatory action should be legally null and void.

Recommendation 3

In the case of partial direct takings, and as regards compensation, the decrease or increase in value should be defined in a net manner, taking into account both the harm and the potential from a regulatory action. Conceivably, such an action might devalue part of a property through a regulatory taking while causing another part of the property to increase in value.

Rationale

In terms of value, both the harm and benefit to use of property (and the value reduction or increase) should be calculated on a net basis. After all, if a city designates part of a piece of farmland for a future industrial park, and thus raises the value of the plot, it is reasonable to count that new use and increased property value against any negative regulatory takings to arrive at a net compensation figure. This follows on the German model (Schmidt-Eichstadt in Alterman, 2010: 274).

Recommendation 4

Compensation levels should account for the effect of the old regulation versus the new, and the difference between old and new plans.

Rationale

In the case of regulation or land planning changes, a determination should be made as to whether the old regulation or old land planning designation is any more or less harmful to value than the new regulation or designation. For example, if the old bylaw requires conservation of a part of some property for ecological reasons (and presumably compensation is paid), while a subsequent and replacement bylaw removes that reason but requires part of the same property to be preserved for aesthetic reasons, no new infringement on use has occurred. This approach would avoid specious claims and it follows on the German model (Schmidt-Eichstadt in Alterman, 2010: 274).

Recommendation 5

When property use is newly restricted, compensation should be offered where the value of the property has fallen 5 percent or more as a result of the change in regulation or plans.

Rationale

Poland compensates for takings "at the first zloty," whereas Israel compensates where a decline in property values has been greater than 1 to 3 percent (Alterman, 2010: 334). In a recent court case in Finland, property owners unable to cut down trees for their forestry business were compensated when restricted use of their land meant its value had declined by 4 percent (Katri Nuuja and Kauko Viitanen in Alterman, 2010: 177). In the United States, depending on the court judgment and/or the state in question, losses must be severely high, 100 percent in some cases, before compensation for regulatory harm can be claimed (Thomas Roberts in Alterman, 2010: 215-227). The American model is the outlier and Canada should follow the European guidelines and compensate when usage has led to a decline in property values of 5 percent or more. Sensible caveats should apply including that property transferred among family members be ineligible and independent valuations be performed.

Property rights and why they matter—theory and literature

"The two ships symbolized this tale of the two Americas. On one, conquistadors; on the other, indentured servants. One group dreamt of instant plunder—of mountains of Mayan gold, there for the taking. The others knew that they had years of toil ahead of them, but also that they would be rewarded with one of the world's most attractive assets— prime North American land—plus a share in the process of law-making. Real estate plus representation: that was the North American dream."
—Niall Ferguson in *Civilization: The West and the Rest* (2011: 98–99)

A short history of property rights theory

That property rights are defensible in and of themselves has long been recognized, at least in Western societies. For example, in England, selected rights that pertained to the individual and his property were recognized as deserving explicit royal protection. In 1215, at the demand of barons, England's King John agreed to guarantee selected rights and liberties in law, and thus to bind himself and his heirs to the rule of law. The result was the constitutional document, the *Magna Carta*. That the early English believed in property rights is evident from one section from that document, where in the case of land inherited by a minor, but temporarily assigned to a guardian, the land was to be delivered to the heir in the condition the guardian received it:

> The keeper of the land of such an heir who is under age is only to take reasonable receipts from the heir's land and reasonable customs and reasonable services, and this without destruction or waste of men or

things. And if we assign custody of any such land to a sheriff or to anyone else who should answer to us for the issues, and such a person should commit destruction or waste, we will take recompense from him … (US National Archives, 1215/1297/2007: 4)

One of the first theorists to lay the groundwork for a comprehensive understanding of private property, and thus the rights derived from the same, was the 17th century Englishman, John Locke. In the *Second Treatise of Government*, originally published in 1690, Locke noted that no one had private property to begin with. There was no private dominion exclusive of the rest of mankind: "The earth, and all that is therein is given to men for the support of their being that is in it, the fruits, vegetables and game, were given to all by God for their support and comfort" (Locke 1690/1997: 17).

This natural arrangement, however, is not where the matter ends. While nature provides a bounty, there must be some justifiable way to appropriate and divide what exists in the commons before it can be of any use to any particular man. After all, Locke reasons in conjunction with this point, nature provides apples on a tree, but left alone, the fruit is merely available, but not yet useful. Left alone, the apples will ripen, fall, and then rot if some intervening action does not take place.

Critically then, the intervention that serves as the linchpin between availability and usefulness is labour (Locke, 1690/1997: 18). And that is how private property is created: labour is annexed to "something" and that "something" becomes his and other men are excluded from it. It is right there that the point of point of private possession occurs: The apples gathered became the property of the picker.

Locke notes that this justification of private property works not only in theory but in practice. He gives several examples: no man suffers because another picks fruit; similarly, no one seriously thinks that those who draw water from a well are not entitled to own and use the water privately; also, it is obvious that a native who kills a deer makes it his because he is the one who has made the effort, who has hunted the deer[1] (Locke, 1690/1997: 18–19).

---

1 An objection can be raised here that this theory of labour justifies hoarding. Locke answers that it does not. Nature sets a limit on what we can make private because fruit, vegetables, and killed meat spoils. Nature sets a limit. This is "God's way" of telling us to exercise dominion responsibly, according to Locke (Locke, 1690/1997: 19).

This applies not only to consumable items such as fruit and vegetables or hunted animals, but also to land itself. Here, Locke anticipates an objection to private property rights exercised over land. It might be argued that land, unlike berries in a forest where only a few people may live and where such supplies then are not exhausted, can be exhausted. There is only so much land.

However, and at first, this does not present a problem. In a lightly populated territory, the needs are limited (you only need so much food for your own family) and thus enclosing some land and making it private is not a barrier to others seeking sustenance. But even when land becomes scarce, this does not change the justification for private property. First, there is the right of property ownership which results from labour, but second, there is the benefit for all others that results when one person works their land and which can ultimately produce wider benefits (Locke, 1690/1997: 18–30).

To use a modern example from Canada's settlement period, ten acres of land in a fertile valley will still only have so many berries on it if left alone to grow naturally. Moreover, if everyone picks those berries, it may provide only a meagre sustenance. However, if that land is enclosed and corn is planted on it, and then sold, everyone benefits. To use a modern example, the town physician who tends to the sick, or an auto mechanic who fixes cars, are not likely to have time to tend to their own gardens, at least not on a full-time basis. They can instead trade their services or buy corn with cash. This is what Locke means when he writes that the private landowner's labour does not lessen, but rather increases the common stock of mankind. It is an early argument about how the division of labour occurs and how such division combined with private property rights creates more goods than would otherwise be available if everyone had to tend to their own ten-acre plot of land with fruit, vegetables, and livestock.

Also, the notion that extra *property* cannot be created is false. While more *land* is rarely created (in the case of extending a shoreline, for example), more physical and other property is created on a daily basis: the construction of a condominium building may create 10, 20, or 200 extra units of housing. Intellectually, new patents are filed every day around the world for the protection of that sort of newly-created property.

It is critical to remember that all such property is akin to real land (and vice-versa) to its owner for the purposes of wealth creation: A retired teacher may own two houses and use one for rental income so as to supplement her retirement pension; a doctor may choose to invest only in blue chip stocks that pay a dividend in order to use the money for part of his daughter's tuition expenses; a soon-to-be-retired farming couple may desire to subdivide their land and use the proceeds to fund their retirement. In each instance, the exact type of private property matters not in terms of its ability to help the individual and his or her family. What matters is that governments not artificially damage the value of such property through ill-advised laws or regulations—at least not without proper compensation.

To summarize, Locke's justification of private property is that labour first creates the right to private property; second, ultimately, private land is more productive than common land; third, that many more people then benefit from this arrangement as a result: there are more goods. The economic pie has grown. It is thus critical that interference in that process be properly compensated.

There is another distinct rationale for property rights: the promotion of freedom. The argument is that, without property, the ability to advance one's idea of the "good life" and exercise all the other rights such as expression is diminished. Charles Reich in his 1964 *Yale Law Journal* article, "The New Property" (1964: 771) notes that one of the functions of property is "to draw a boundary [between] public and private power," inside which the state must justify and explain any interference. Reich also argues that the right to hold property enables one to enjoy other rights, such as the right to control one's destiny, the right to not be reliant on the state (except to the extent needed to ensure the enforcement of property rights and selected other enforcements). Amartya Sen makes a similar argument for the necessity of property rights to the good life in *Development as Freedom*, and the Fraser Institute's *Economic Freedom of the World* notes how strong property rights beget freedom, and vice-versa (Gwartney et al., 2011: 6).

The general empirical case for property rights: An overview

Property rights are a critical component in the development of a prosperous and thriving economy. Clearly defined and protected property rights encourage economic growth through several channels; strong property rights promote efficient market exchange, productive investment, and entrepreneurial risk taking. Strong property rights also reduce transaction and contract costs, protect individuals and businesses from unlawful expropriation, and promote social trust and harmony. Lastly, property rights help place the costs of a desired activity on those want the activity—not on the property owner—and thus avoiding what economists call the "free-ridership" problem whereby some individuals derive benefit from the expenditures of others.

For example, this author likes to hike. It would be wrong of government to require private landowners to build or even allow access trails or hiking paths on their land—and offer no compensation. If the public desires the public use of private land, for any purpose, compensation from the public treasury must be forthcoming, just as if a private interest wishes to rent someone's house for a film shoot, the film company would pay for access.

How property rights create wealth

An important difference that separates many relatively wealthy economies from other less developed and relatively poor economies is the strength of legislative and judicial protections for property rights. An abundance of empirical findings support the assertion that fully delineated and secure property rights promote economic growth and the efficient allocation of scarce resources through well-functioning markets (O'Driscoll, 2003; Asoni, 2008). Furthermore, numerous studies have investigated and identified the precise mechanisms or channels through which secure property rights promote economic growth (Barro, 1991, 1997; Knack and Keefer, 1995, 1997; Heitger, 2003; Dincer, 2007; Scully, 1988; Grier and Tullock, 1989; Gwartney et al., 2004, 2006).

Those growth-promoting mechanisms and channels include the positive impact of secure property rights for increasing savings and productive investment (Barro, 2000; Dincer, 2007), creating incentives for technological innovation, reducing transaction and contractual costs (North, 1991; Barzel, 1987), reducing economic predation and corruption (Mauro, 1995; O'Driscoll, 2003), and correcting various manifestations of market externalities such as free ridership (Coase, 1960; Pasour, 1981; Stroup and Baden, 1979).

In contrast, countries where property rights are subject to unrestrained alienation are typically plagued by less than optimal levels of savings and investment, a shortage of innovative activity, relatively high transaction costs, pervasive market externalities, and systematic economic corruption, preda-tion, and rent seeking. In sum, a secure property rights regime (both pri-vate and public) is essential for promoting productive economic [business] activity, efficient market exchange, and national economic development (Barro, 1991, 1997, 2000; O'Driscoll, 2003; Dincer, 2007; Asoni, 2008).

A key observation about the importance of property rights for properly functioning markets was made by Nobel Laureate Ronald Coase (1960) who demonstrated that market failures can be abated if property rights are well-defined, secure, and easily transferable. Furthermore, Professor Coase showed that a resource will be put to its most valuable use if property rights protecting that resource, irrespective of the original assignment of those rights, are well defined, secure, and easily transferable (Coase, 1960).

The linkage between secure property rights and economic growth has been well-established empirically. Two prominent studies by Economist Robert Barro analyzing 100 countries between 1960 and 1990[2] concluded that the "rule of law" and restrained government enhance economic growth (Barro, 1991, 1997, 2000). Another insightful study by Knack and Keefer (1995) used indices of country-by-country investment risk as prox-ies for institutions that safeguard property rights and found evidence of a link between secure property rights, business investment, physical capital accumulation, and national economic growth. Johan Tortensson (1994) used the degree of state ownership in the economy and the susceptibility of private property owners to arbitrary expropriation as proxies for the security of property rights. He found that the extent of state ownership in the economy does not significantly affect economic growth, while height-ened risk of arbitrary expropriation of private property discernibly reduces economic growth.

Two similar studies by Bernhard Hietger (2003) and Oguzhan Dincer (2007) explicitly introduce property rights protection into traditional models of economic growth. Hietger (2003) analyzed a selection of coun-tries between 1975 and 1995 and concluded that secure property rights had a discernable positive impact on national prosperity and economic efficiency. Similarly, Dincer (2007) looked at 79 countries for the period 1982 to 1997 and found that the accumulation of both human and physical

---

2   The second study by Barro (1997) also analyzed roughly 100 countries but over a shorter period, from 1965 to 1990.

capital, and the corresponding level of economic output (per capita Gross Domestic Product), were positively related to the degree of property rights protection. He also found that the effect of the national savings rate on the level of economic output was also positively correlated with the security of property rights (Dincer, 2007).

An assortment of other studies have used measures of political, economic, and civil freedoms to establish a link between secure property rights and economic growth including Scully (1988), Grier and Tullock (1989), and Gwartney et al. (2004).

To be clear, on measures of property rights, Canada ranks relatively high in comparison to other countries (15th out of 141 jurisdictions in Gwartney et al., 2011: 10). Thus, Canada is already in the "model class" that demonstrates how secure access to property and its retention and use create prosperity. In that sense, added constitutional protection would not be a "revolutionary" wealth creator in the manner that the introduction of even basic property such rights would be in say, Zimbabwe or Cuba. However, improvements in Canada's protection of property rights could, in the future, protect individual Canadians and their families from new and old forms of takings that devalue their property. Conversely, there is always the risk that a lack of constitutional protection for property rights could erode property rights significantly and that in the long term would have a negative effect on prosperity. The question of possible constitutional protection will be addressed in more depth in Appendix C of this book.

Property rights and technological innovation

Promoting technological innovation is another essential feature of secure property rights in enabling economic development. In fact, the "Copyright Clause" of the US Constitution clearly aims at this end and is written as follows: "To promote the Progress of Science and useful Arts, by securing for limited Times to Authors and Inventors the exclusive Right to their respective Writings and Discoveries" (US Constitution: Article 1, Section 8, Clause 8).

Secure property rights encourage innovation by enabling the developers of new technologies, improved operational methods, novel business ideas, and various other market-enhancing efficiencies to protect the potential returns to their investment in resources, materials, and time, if their innovation ultimately proves to be a commercial success (Supreme

Court of the United States, 2002; Landes and Posner, 1989; Committee for Economic Development, 2004). Conversely, systematic vulnerability and unrestrained alienation of private property rights jeopardizes the potential rewards to entrepreneurship, business risk taking, and technological innovation.

The effect on poverty

The link between secure property rights as a social institution and economic growth was underscored in the seminal work Nobel Laureate Douglass North. North (1990, 1991) highlighted property rights protection as one of the critical institutional differences that made possible the industrial revolution in Western Europe and contributed to a global divergence between modern developed and underdeveloped economies, a divergence that has yet to be eliminated. The role of secure property in explaining the historical divergence in global living standards over the past several centuries was further emphasized in the extensive and influential contribution of Daron Acemoglu and several of his co-authors (Acemoglu, 2005a, 2005b; Acemoglu and Verdier, 1998; Acemoglu and Robinson, 2000; Acemoglu and Johnson, 2005; Acemoglu et al., 2001, 2002, 2005). Acemoglu and his co-authors used several proxies to offer a historical explanation of why secure property rights regimes arose in certain societies and settlements, and were relatively neglected by other societies in other geographic locales[3] during modern history.

The insecurity of property rights has been linked to extreme poverty in underdeveloped countries (Norton, 1998). Conversely, in the modern globalized economy, secure property rights can promote economic growth in developing countries by allowing unused and underused capital

---

3   More specifically, Acemoglu and his coauthors (Acemoglu and Robinson, 2000; Acemoglu and Johnson, 2005; Acemoglu et al., 2001, 2002, 2005) have argued that based on geographic conditions, colonialists from the preeminent European empires of the 17th through to 20th century and Great Britain faced different incentives regarding the creation of secure property rights. Some geographic locales were more suited to economic predation because of inhospitable environments, and in such locales property rights were mostly neglected. Other more hospitable environments that were characterized by a relatively high dispersion of productive resources were also more naturally conducive to economic cooperation and market exchange. In these relatively favorable environments colonialists faced much stronger incentives to establish and protect private property rights.

to be infused into the formal economy and channeled towards productive investment. Hernando de Soto (1989, 2000) has posited that many developing countries already possess an extensive stock of potentially productive capital that could be put to use more effectively if property rights were better defined and protected (by legislation and an independent judiciary). Conversely, insecure property rights can constrain economic growth by reducing the gains from trade, increasing the risk of appropriation, keeping capital idle or unproductive, creating a need for property owners to waste resources defending against predation, and limiting the extent to which property can be used as collateral to finance productive investment (Besley and Ghatak, 2009).

How property rights help the environment

Well-defined and secure property rights also provide a powerful incentive for the preservation of natural resources, without which the tragedy of the commons is in play. Property rights are also important for determining the most effective use of natural resources. As such, properly defining and vigilantly protecting property rights is likely to create considerable economic and environmental benefits (Stroup and Baden, 1979; Anderson and Leal, 2001; Stroup, 2008).

Private property rights have two complementary implications: they protect the rights of owners to use and dispose of property in accordance with their personal tastes and preferences, but they also oblige non-interference with, and respect for, other people's rights to use and benefit from their own property. As such, well defined and secure property rights are essential for resolving disputes about the use of natural resources, protecting the environment, and limiting the amount of pollution and emissions to socially optimal levels (Field and Olewiler, 2001; Anderson and Leal, 2001; Stroup, 2008).

Legal disputes related to pollution and environmental preservation are settled typically within the judicial framework of trespass law or nuisance law and often invoke considerations of riparian rights.[4] When pollution

---

4　"Riparian" refers to the interplay between those who possess land and are close to a body of water. The general principle is that landowners whose property abuts a body of water have the right to make reasonable use of that water. Riparian water rights are thus the system for allocating such water in the event that there is not enough to satisfy all users.

results in a direct and tangible infringement on the property rights of other individuals, trespass law is the standard framework for adjudication. When pollution results in indirect or less tangible infringements on the use or enjoyment of private property, nuisance law becomes the standard framework for adjudication.

Stronger property rights could provide individuals with the tools to safeguard the resources on which their material well-being depends. Furthermore, strengthened property rights would create powerful incentives for businesses to reduce emissions and other environmentally degrading operations (Anderson and Leal, 2001; Stroup, 2008). Property rights are an essential component in any effort to protect the environment. Well defined and secure property rights can promote environmental conservation by giving owners an incentive to avoid depleting or degrading their resources beyond the optimal level. Secure property rights ensure that natural resource owners are fully compensated for the use of their land, water, and air. In sum, property rights are a crucial component of any initiative aimed at improving environmental protection (Field and Olewiler, 2001; Anderson and Leal, 2001; Stroup, 2008).

Although the empirical literature linking the security of property rights to environmental protection is relatively limited, one recent study analyzing a selection of countries to determine the effect of property rights protection on environmental quality found that environmental quality and environmental protection is superior in those countries where property rights are well defined and protected, especially with regards to property rights over natural resources such as land and water (Kerekes, 2011).

Canada's history of property rights

> *"Even as the West prospers from abundant capital, do people really understand the origin of capital? If they don't, there always remains the possibility the West might damage the source of its own strength."*
> Hernando de Soto, in *The Mystery of Capital* (2000: 8)

Property rights in Canadian and colonial history

Canada has a long pre- and post-Confederation tradition of respect for property rights. It is worth a brief look at selected statements from a few of Canada's past leaders, who saw such rights as integral to Canada's well-being.

In 1865, George-Étienne Cartier, then a legislator in the Legislature of Canada, attempted to reassure fellow Canadians about the then-proposed federation project. He especially tried to reassure English Canadians that the (French) customary laws that had prevailed in Lower Canada would not stand in the way of the protection of property rights in that province should the union of the provinces into Confederation succeed. Historically, the customary laws in Lower Canada and some anti-commercial sentiment in Lower Canada (the geographic and political region later to become Quebec and Labrador) combined to present a barrier to commercial enterprise.

However, the anti-commercial nature of Lower Canada (noted above and pointed to by historian Janet Ajzenstat [Ajzenstat, Romney, Gentles, and Gairdner, 1999: 335]) had dissipated somewhat after the abolition of the Lower Canadian Legislature by the union of 1840 (of Lower and Upper Canada), the rise of commercially-minded francophone bourgeoisie, and the codification of civil law between 1859 and 1866. Thus, by 1865, while noting the concern over the past orientation and customary law, Cartier remarked in legislative debates over the future proposed federation that,

There could be no reason for well-grounded fear that the minority could be made to suffer by means of any laws affecting the rights of property. If any such enactments were passed, they would fall upon the whole community. But even supposing such a thing did occur, there was a remedy provided in the proposed constitution.[1] (Ajzenstat, 1999: 335)

Similarly, Joseph-François Armand, a representative on Canada's Legislative Council (from 1858 to 1867), encouraged legislators to preserve the spirit of the "mother country's" established Constitution, one "established after centuries of efforts and contests." Armand specifically refers to property as one of Canadians' "sacred rights" (Ajzenstat, 1999: 91).

Later, in a 1940 Report of the Royal Commission on Dominion-Provincial Relations, the commission reflects on the original intent of the Quebec Act of 1774, and how it was designed to safeguard the cultural autonomy of Quebec. With reference to the phrase "Property and Civil Rights in the Province," the commission notes how it has a long history in British North America, "rising out of the relationships of the French and English in the valley of the St. Lawrence."

More specifically, and quoting the Quebec Act of 1774, the authors note that its reference to securing "'His Majesty's Canadian [Quebec] subjects within the province of Quebec' in the enjoyment of their property and civil rights and provided that 'in all matters of controversy relative to property and civil rights, resort shall be had to the laws of Canada as the rule for the decision of the same'" (Canada, 1940: 34).

In the historical cases just noted, the clear and common link between them is how Canada's pre- and post-Confederation legislators explicitly assumed that property rights were worthwhile and deserving of protection. (This was also part of a larger tug-of-war between the federal government, which saw the provinces as potential usurpers of property rights, and provincial legislatures, which jealously protected their jurisdiction under s. 92(13) (16–18)).

More recently, Prime Minister John Diefenbaker was a strong proponent of civil rights, including property rights. In a 1950 speech, seven

---

1   The reference is to the disallowance and reservation powers, then proposed for the federal government, and indeed now found in Sections 55 through 57, and 90 of the Constitution Act, 1867.

years before he became prime minister, and as a Member of Parliament for a Saskatchewan riding, Diefenbaker made clear his preference for a Canadian Bill of Rights (CBC, 1950). One decade later, that Bill of Rights was eventually enacted by Parliament, in 1960, with Diefenbaker now prime minister. Among its provisions was section 1a, "the right of the individual to life, liberty, security of the person and enjoyment of property, and the right not to be deprived thereof except by due process of law" (Canada, 1960).[2]

Attempts to entrench property rights in the Constitution

The government that followed, the Liberal government of Lester Pearson, also attempted to strengthen Canada's property rights regime, this time on a constitutional basis. In 1968, then Justice Minister Pierre Trudeau proposed giving certain rights constitutional protection, including property. One year later, as the Library of Parliament notes, "in 1969, as prime minister, Mr. Trudeau again proposed entrenchment of a charter of rights which would have guaranteed the right of an individual to use and enjoy property, with the assurance that there would be no deprivation of property except in accordance with proper legal procedures" (Johansen, 1991).

That later attempt failed as part of a broader failure to achieve constitutional reform in 1971, and property rights as a constitutional issue was again off the table until 1978, when Bill C-60, the Constitutional Amendment Bill, proposed the following language be added to Canada's Constitution: the right of the individual to the use and enjoyment of property, and the right not to be deprived thereof except in accordance with law (Johansen, 1991).

Most provinces opposed to the proposed constitutional change on the grounds that their land regulations could be nullified. (In fact, only British Columbia supported it.) In response, the federal government noted the amendment was somewhat weak, since it only required that a deprivation "be in accordance with law." Still, in response to concerns from the provinces, the federal government re-wrote the property rights proposal for a 1980 meeting between the premiers and prime minister. The new proposed language was as follows, in a proposed Section 9:

---

2   Still, given the Bill of Rights was a statute, this is not to suggest it has the equivalent weight of a constitution.

1. Everyone has the right to the use and enjoyment of property, individually or in association with others, and the right not to be deprived thereof except in accordance with law and for reasonable compensation.

2. Nothing in this section precludes the enactment of or renders invalid laws controlling or restricting the use of property in the public interest or securing against property the payment of taxes or duties or other levies or penalties. (Johansen 1991)

This compromise proposal still failed and the Liberal government of Pierre Trudeau decided to postpone the issue of property rights protection to the next round of constitutional negotiations in 1981. In the interim, the federal Progressive Conservative party proposed this amendment to section 7 of the Constitution (which already guaranteed basic rights):

> Everyone has the right to life, liberty, security of the person and enjoyment of property and the right not to be deprived thereof except in accordance with the principles of fundamental justice. (Johansen, 1991)

Still, and even though the federal government was willing to accept this amendment, Prince Edward Island refused. Also, the federal New Democratic Party, although not holding the balance of power in Parliament, opposed any property rights protection unless so-called economic and social rights were also given constitutional status. The final draft of the proposed Canadian Charter of Rights and Freedoms thus had no mention of property rights. This is the current state today and despite several parliamentary attempts since to further the issue, including in 1983 and 1987 (Johansen, 1991).

Remedies to the existing constitutional omissions

> "The basic law where the protection of property rights is anchored was enacted in 1992. By that time, civil rights in general and, among them, property rights had been well established through the 'unwritten constitution'. Long before Basic Law: Human Dignity and Liberty was enacted in 1992, the Supreme Court repeatedly recognized property rights as holding 'constitutional status'."
>
> Rachelle Alterman on Israel's property rights protection
> in *Takings International* (2010: 315)

The straightforward unwillingness of governments to compensate Canadians for regulatory infringements on their property and the absence of property rights in Canada's Constitution makes evident the need to address such omissions in Canadian public policy. In this section, however, I examine the constitutional possibilities for more entrenched property rights protection, and which could conceivably cover existing recognized rights to compensation (expropriation) and future (regulatory takings).

As constitutional expert Warren Newman writes in a 2007 article for *Supreme Court Law Review*, Part V of the Constitution Act, 1982, contains five procedures for amending the Constitution of Canada:

> They range from the very difficult—section 41, the so-called "unanimity" formula, requiring the consent of the Senate, the House of Commons, and all 10 provincial legislative assemblies—to the relatively facile—section 45, one of the two "unilateral" procedures; requiring, in this instance, the approval of only one legislative body. The "general,"

or default procedure, is to be found in section 38; it is the amending formula that applies when none of the other procedures (in section 41, 43, 44 or 45) does. It is also the procedure that is required to be used for amendments in relation to the matters specified in section 42. (Newman, 2007: 387)

In my review of constitutional possibilities, I will examine sections 43 and 45, with the former the subject of at least one existing attempt to amend the Constitution for property rights protection. First, some history on previous attempts:

Constitutional possibilities

In his 1960 address to Parliament the day previous to the introduction of his Canadian Bill of Rights, Prime Minister Diefenbaker was aware that some would criticize it as "mere" legislation; they would have preferred to give such rights, including property rights, constitutional status. He agreed:

> There are, of course, those who say that the bill in its present form does not go far enough—that it should be a constitutional amendment binding on Parliament and the legislatures. To do this would require the consent of all the provinces, and that is not attainable as yet. This bill will, however, cover all matters within the jurisdiction of the Federal Parliament. (Diefenbaker, 1960)

However, as detailed in the previous section, multiple attempts over the last five decades have failed to either amend an existing section of the Constitution, or introduce a new section outright, that would protect property rights. In part, since 1982, that is due to the high hurdle necessary for any constitutional amendment to take effect: passage by the federal Parliament and Senate and seven out of ten provinces that constitute at least 50 percent of the population (Canada, Department of Justice, undated a: Section 38 (1) (2)).

While passage of a constitutional amendment to protect property should not be forsworn as a desirable end, a nearer-term strategy is for the federal Parliament and at least one provincial legislature to pass a motion in favour of property rights that applies to that willing province.

Constitutionally, this is possible through the use of sections 43 and 45 (with the limitations noted by section 41).[1] Sections 43 and 45 are as follows:

Amendment of provisions relating to some but not all provinces

43. An amendment to the Constitution of Canada in relation to any provision that applies to one or more, but not all, provinces, including

  (a) any alteration to boundaries between provinces, and

  (b) any amendment to any provision that relates to the use of the English or the French language within a province may be made by proclamation issued by the Governor General under the Great Seal of Canada only where so authorized by resolutions of the Senate and House of Commons and of the legislative assembly of each province to which the amendment applies.

Amendments by provincial legislatures

45. Subject to section 41, the legislature of each province may exclusively make laws amending the constitution of the province (Canada, Department of Justice, undated b).

Precedent for provincial-federal amendments to the Constitution under section 43

There have been amendments to the constitution that bind a specific province using section 43 of the Constitution. They are as follows:

Constitution Amendment, 1987 (Newfoundland Act)   This act entrenched the denominational school rights of the Pentecostal Assemblies of Newfoundland (and was repealed by a subsequent amendment in 1998). This amendment was made using the section 43 amending formula (Parliament and the Newfoundland Legislature).

Constitution Amendment, 1993 (New Brunswick)   Established the equality of the English-speaking and French-speaking communities in New Brunswick.

---

1   Section 41 limits any amendment to the Constitution as it concerns the monarchy, Senate representation for provinces, the composition of the Supreme Court of Canada, the use of the French language, and alterations to section 41 itself, to a unanimous declaration of all provinces and Parliament.

Constitution Amendment, 1994 (Prince Edward Island) This act relieved Canada of the obligation to provide ferry service to Prince Edward Island upon completion of the Confederation Bridge and was made using the section 43 amending formula (Parliament and the Prince Edward Island Legislature).

Constitution Amendment, 1997 (Quebec) This Act permitted Quebec school boards to be restructured on linguistic lines, rather than on a denominational basis and was made using the section 43 amending formula (Parliament and the Quebec Legislature).

Constitution Amendment Act, 1997 (Newfoundland Act) This allowed the province to create a secular school system and was made using the section 43 amending formula (Parliament and the Newfoundland Legislature).

Constitution Amendment Proclamation, 1998 (Newfoundland) This proclamation allowed the province to abolish the denominational school system and was made using the section 43 amending formula (Parliament and the Newfoundland Legislature).

Constitution Amendment, 2001 (Newfoundland and Labrador) Amended Newfoundland's Terms of Union to change the province's name to "Newfoundland and Labrador" and was made using the section 43 amending formula (Parliament and the Newfoundland Legislature).

(All above references: Privy Council Office, undated.)

Section 43 and its applicability to property rights

Thus, a novel possibility in the pursuit of protected property rights is for a provincial legislature, in cooperation with Parliament, to amend the federal Constitution to protect property rights within that province. This has already been conceived of by at least two politicians: In February 2011, Ontario Conservative Member of Parliament Scott Reid, and Randy Hillier, Member of the Provincial Parliament in Ontario, announced their intention to jointly present resolutions in the House of Commons and the Legislative Assembly of Ontario to amend Canada's Constitution to embed property rights within the Charter of Rights and Freedoms. As of late 2011, the intention was to present such resolutions in 2012 (Hillier, 2011). The proposed amendment would use section 43 to amend section 7 and insert the following:

> 7.1 (1) In Ontario, everyone has the right not to be deprived, by any act of the Legislative Assembly or by any action taken under authority of an act of the Legislative Assembly, of the title, use, or enjoyment of real property or of any right attached to real property, or of any improvement made to or upon real property, unless made whole by means of full, just, and timely financial compensation. (2) Subsection (1) refers to any act of the Legislative Assembly made before or after the coming into force of this section. (Reid, 2011)

In discussing their amendment, Reid notes that it is "carefully crafted to be as limited as possible" and "deals only with real property (i.e., real estate) and improvements made to that property. It does not deal with patents, copyright, trademarks, or any other form of non-material property. It also does nothing to protect property in moveable objects." Further,

> the amendment is also designed so as not to limit the ability of the Ontario Legislature to pass laws that strip away property rights; both Randy and I believe that restrictions on private property can, on many occasions, serve the public interest. Our only concern is that when an action is designed to benefit the public—by protecting watercourses or endangered species, by creating greenbelt areas, etc.—it is the public which should pay the associated costs, just as the public would pay if a direct expropriation of the title to the land were taking place. (Reid, 2011)

Thus, the proposed amendment does not extend as far as protecting all property. Nor does it necessarily guarantee that governments cannot interfere with private property, including expropriation and regulatory actions. On the face of it, it does, in fact, address a property rights infringement not now covered by common law and the main focus topic of this paper: regulatory takings.

Questions about the usefulness of section 43 in this exercise

However, it should be noted that at least one legal scholar questions the possibility for section 43 to be used to amend the Constitution, even as applicable to one province, unless the amendment in question concerns an existing provision (that applies to less than all provinces) and is not an attempt to amend the Constitution (for less than all provinces) on a new matter.

Warren Newman writes:

> The key [that opens] the door to the use of section 43 is a provision of the Constitution of Canada that applies to one or more, but not all, provinces. Once one ... [such provision is present]—for example, the provisions of section 93 of the Constitution Act, 1867, relating to denominational and separate schools, which do not apply to all provinces—then in principle, section 43 of the Constitution Act, 1982 is available. (Newman, 2007: 389)

In other words, Newman takes the view that section 43 can only be used to amend an existing provision that applies to less than all provinces, not to introduce a new provision that will apply to less than all provinces. The existing uses of section 43 listed above all conform to this understanding.

The Reid/Hillier proposal with respect to section 7 would mark a new departure in the sense of adding a new provision applicable to only one province. It is possible to read section 43 to allow that—and it may well be tested in court if the amendment passes the Ontario Legislature and the federal Parliament—but in the meantime, those in pursuit of the attempt should be aware of the hurdle that such a reading would have to clear.

Section 45 as another option for property rights protection

Section 45 may well be another option for those who wish to see property rights as a protected category within the Constitution. Section 45 replaces the "old" section 92 (1) and Newman also addresses it in his 2007 work, asserting that Section 45:

> ... does not include the power to circumvent the role of the Lieutenant-Governor in the legislative process, or to abrogate a constitutional provision essential to the operation of federalism nor a fundamental term

of union, such as section 133 of the Constitution Act, 1867 or section 23 of the Manitoba Act, 1870 (which protect the use of English and French in the legislature and courts); and it does not include a power to "bring about profound constitutional upheaval by the introduction of political institutions foreign to and incompatible with the Canadian system..." (Newman, 2007: 390-92)

With the above caveats on section 45 in mind, another constitutional scholar, Professor Rainer Knopff, considers that some may argue that the precedents noted all pertain to the operation of government, not to substantive rights protections, and that such a "fundamental" revision of section 7—especially since property rights were explicitly left out of the Charter—is beyond the scope of section 45. Knopff notes that is likely a weak argument, but that "weak arguments have on occasion won the day" (Knopff, February 21, 2012, personal e-mail correspondence with author). University of Toronto professor scholar Nelson Wiseman notes that provincial constitutions are no longer considered entirely outside the British North America Act (Wiseman, 2008: 138), which would seem to give succor to those who would use sections 43 or 45 to create a constitutional property rights protection.

In 1984, Campbell Sharman, anticipating the possibility that provinces may wish to reform their constitutions and that those incremental moves using existing provisions may achieve such an end, wrote:

> Provinces may wish to reform their constitutions, not by making substantive changes but by attempting to restate constitutional rules and clarifying existing law. This might take the form of no more than a carefully thought through consolidation of existing acts to create a document with internal coherence worthy of the name of constitution. Or, more ambitiously it might involve an attempt to express broader constitutional principles either by appending explicatory preambles or by reducing matters at present left to convention to statements of positive law. (Sharman, 1984: 106–107)

Also, Sharman explicitly mentions entrenching property rights as one such possible reform and through the avenue of super-majorities in both the legislature and a referenda process (1984: 108).

On the question of whether such super-majorities or referenda would constitute a "profound upheaval," yet another constitutional scholar, Ted Morton weighs in. He notes how some scholars see severe restrictions on section 45 use (Newman's comments above would be an example), this due to the clause that powers to amend provincial constitutions (such as they are) do not include the power to "bring about profound constitutional upheaval by the introduction of political institutions foreign to and incompatible with the Canadian system." However, Morton points out that "neither entrenched rights nor a super-majoritarian amending formula are foreign to Canada… [The provinces] would just be doing what Ottawa has already done," citing past examples of both practices at both the federal and provincial levels (Morton, 2004: 3).

In short, both section 43 and section 45 may allow for the possibility of stretching constitutional protection beyond existing rights clauses to real property if enacted in the manner envisioned by Reid and Hiller. That is not to say such an approach would not be the subject of a test case in the country's courts; it may well be.

References

Acemoglu, Daron (2005a). *Modeling Inefficient Institutions*. Working Paper no. 11940. National Bureau of Economic Resarch (NBER).

Acemoglu, Daron (2005b). *The Form of Property Rights: Oligarchic versus Democratic Societies*. Working Paper no. 10037. National Bureau of Economic Resarch (NBER).

Acemoglu, D., and S. Johnson (2005). Unbundling institutions. *Journal of Political Economy* 113, 5: 949–95.

Acemoglu, D., and J. Robinson (2000). Democratization or Repression? *European Economic Review* 44, 4–6: 683–93.

Acemoglu, D., and T. Verdier (1998). Property Rights, Corruption and the Allocation of Talent: A General Equilibrium Approach. *Economic Journal* 108, 450: 1381–403.

Acemoglu, D., S. Johnson, and J. Robinson (2001). Colonial Origins of Comparative Development: An Empirical Investigation. *American Economic Review* 91, 5: 1369–401.

Acemoglu, D., S. Johnson, and J. Robinson (2002). Reversal of Fortune: Geography and Institutions in the Making of the Modern World Income Distribution. *Quarterly Journal of Economics* 117, 4: 1231–94.

Acemoglu, D., S. Johnson, and J. Robinson (2005). The Rise of Europe: Atlantic Trade, Institutional Change and Economic Growth. *American Economic Review* 95, 3: 546–79.

Ajzenstat, Janet, Paul Romney, Ian Gentles, and William Gairdner (1999). *Canada's Founding Debates*. Stoddart.

Alterman, Rachelle (2010). *Takings International: A Comparative Perspective on Land Use Regulations and Compensation Rights*. American Bar Association.

Anderson, T.L., and D.R. Leal (2001). *Free Market Environmentalism*. Palgrave.

Asoni, Andrea (2008). Protection of Property Rights and Growth as Political Equilibria. *Journal of Economic Surveys* 22, 5 (December): 953–87.

Barro, Robert (1991). Economic Growth in a Cross Section of Countries. *Quarterly Journal of Economics* 106, 2: 407–43.

Barro, Robert J. (1997). *Determinants of Economic Growth: A Cross-Country Empirical Study*. MIT Press.

Barro, Robert J. (2000). Chapter 2: Rule of Law, Democracy, and Economic Performance. *2000 Index of Economic Freedom* (Heritage Foundation): 31–49. <http://geser.net/Barro.pdf>, as of April 4, 2012.

Barzel, Yoram (1989). *Economic Analysis of Property Rights*. Cambridge University Press.

Besley, Timothy J., and Maitreesh Ghatak (2009). *Property Rights and Economic Development*. CEPR Discussion Paper No. DP7243 (March).

Brown, Russell (2007). The Constructive Taking at the Supreme Court of Canada: Once More without Feeling. *University of British Columbia Law Review* 40: 315–42.

Brown, Russell (2011). "Takings": Government Liability to Compensate for Forcibly Acquired Property. In Karen Horsman and Gareth Morley (eds.), *Government Liability: Law and Practice* (Canada Law Book): ch. 4.

Brown, Russell, and Graham Purse (2011). *Regulation of Property Use and Regulatory Takings in Alberta*. Canadian Constitution Foundation. <http://www.canadianconstitutionfoundation.ca/files/24/CCF%20-%20AB%20Regulatory%20Takings%20Paper.pdf>, as of February 27, 2012.

Campbell, Charles (2006). *Forever Farmland: Reshaping the Agricultural Land Reserve for the 21st Century*. David Suzuki Foundation. <http://www.davidsuzuki.org/publications/downloads/2006/DSF-ALR-final3.pdf>, as of December 19, 2011.

Canadian Broadcasting Corporation (1950, March 16). *A Canadian Bill of Rights—A Debate*. <http://www.cbc.ca/archives/categories/politics/prime-ministers/john-diefenbaker-dief-the-chief/the-canadian-bill-of-rights.html>, as of July 15, 2011.

Carss-Fisk, Monica (2001). *The Right to Property: A Guide to the Implementation of Article 1 of Protocol No. 1 to the European Convention on Human Rights*. Human Rights Handbooks no. 4. Council of Europe. <http://echr.coe.int/NR/rdonlyres/AFE5CA8A-9F42-4F6F-997B-12E290BA2121/0/DG2ENHRHAND042003.pdf> as of March 5, 2012.

Carter-Whitney, Maureen (2008). *Ontario's Greenbelt in an International Context: Comparing Ontario's Greenbelt to its Counterparts in Europe and North America*. Friends of the Greenbelt Foundation Occasional Paper Series number 5. Friends of the Greenbelt Foundation. <http://www.cielap.org/pdf/GreenbeltInternationalContext.pdf>, as of March 30, 2012.

Coase, Ronald (1960). The Problem of Social Cost. *Journal of Law and Economics* 3, 1: 1–44.

Committee for Economic Development (2004). *Promoting Innovation and Economic Growth: The Special Problem of Digital Intellectual Property*. Committee for Economic Development. <http://www.immagic.com/eLibrary/GENERAL/CED/C040000H.pdf>, as of April 4, 2012.

de Soto, Hernando (1989). *The Other Path*. Harper and Row.

de Soto, Hernando (2000). *The Mystery of Capital: Why Capitalism Triumphs in the West and Fails Everywhere Else*. Basic Books.

de Soto, Hernando (2009, February 21). Toxic Paper. *Newsweek*. <http://www.newsweek.com/2009/02/20/toxic-paper.html>, as of November 8, 2010.

Diefenbaker, John G. (1960, June 30). Notes for an Address by the Prime Minister, the Right Honourable John G. Diefenbaker, on the "Nation's Business." Library and Archives Canada. <http://www.collectionscanada.gc.ca/2/4/h4-4052-e.html >as of April 4, 2012.

Dincer, Oguzhan C. (2007). The Effects of Property Rights on Economic Performance. *Applied Economics* 39, 7–9 (April-May): 825–37. <http://papers.ssrn.com/sol3/papers.cfm?abstract_id=473361>, as of April 4, 2012.

Epstein, Richard (2005). One Step beyond Nozick's Minimal State: The Role of Forced Exchanges in Political Theory. *Social Philosophy and Political Philosophy* 22, 1: 286–313.

Epstein, Richard. (2008). *Supreme Neglect: How to Revive Constitutional Protection for Private Property*. Oxford University Press.

Ferguson, Niall (2011). *Civilization: The West and the Rest*. Penguin.

Field, Barry, and Nancy Olewiler (2001). *Environmental Economics* (Canadian edition). McGraw-Hill Ryerson Higher Education.

France (1789). *Declaration of the Rights of Man and of the Citizen*. <http://www.britannica.com/bps/additionalcontent/8/116846/Declaration-of-the-Rights-of-Man-and-of-the-Citizen>, as of November 2, 2011.

Grier, K., and Gordon Tullock (1989). An Empirical Analysis of Cross-National Economic Growth, 1951–1980. *Journal of Monetary Economics* 24: 159 –276.

Gwartney, James D., Randall Holcombe, and Robert A. Lawson (2004). Economic Freedom, Institutional Quality, and Cross Country Differences In Income And Growth. *Cato Journal* 24, 3 (Fall): 205–33. <http://www.cato.org/pubs/journal/cj24n3/cj24n3-2.pdf>, as of April 4, 2012.

Gwartney, James D., Randall Holcombe, and Robert A. Lawson (2006). Institutions and the Impact of Investment on Growth. *Kyklos* 59, 2 (May): 255–73.

Gwartney, James D., Robert A. Lawson, and Joshua Hall (2011). *Economic Freedom of the World: 2011 Annual Report.* Fraser Institute. <http://www.freetheworld.com/2011/reports/world/EFW2011_complete.pdf>, as of February 7, 2012.

Heuston, R.F.V. (1977). *Salmond on the Law of Torts*, 17th ed. Sweet & Maxwell.

Hietger, Bernhard (2003). Property Rights and the Wealth of Nations: A Cross Country Study. *Cato Journal* 23, 3: 381–401.

Johansen, David (1991). *Property Rights and the Constitution.* Depository Services Program, Law and Government Division, Government of Canada. <http://dsp-psd.pwgsc.gc.ca/Collection-R/LoPBdP/BP/bp268-e.htm>, as of October 18, 2011.

Kerekes, Carrie (2011). Property Rights and Environmental Quality: A Cross Country Study. *Cato Journal* 31, 2 (Spring-Summer): 315–38.

Knack, S., and P. Keefer (1995). Institutions and Economic Performance: Cross Country Testing Using Alternative Institutional Measures. *Economics and Politics* 7: 207–27.

Knopff, Rainer (2002). Why We Shouldn't Entrench Property Rights. *Policy Options* (July-August). <http://www.irpp.org/po/archive/jul02/knopff.pdf>, as of April 11, 2012.

Landes, William M., and Richard A. Posner (1989). An Economic Analysis of Copyright Law. *Journal of Legal Studies* 18, 2 (June): 325–63.

Locke, John (1997/1690). *The Second Treatise of Government.* Thomas Peardon, ed. Prentice Hall.

Mauro, P. (1995). Corruption and Growth. *Quarterly Journal of Economics* 110, 3: 681–712.

Morton, Ted (2004). Provincial Constitutions in Canada. Paper presented to the conference, Federalism and Sub-national Constitutions: Design and Reform. Center for the Study of State Constitutions. Rockefeller Centre, Bellagio, Italy (March 22–26). <http://camlaw.rutgers.edu/statecon/subpapers/morton.pdf>, as of February 29, 2012.

Moulton, Alexis (2005). Your Role in Expropriation. *Canadian Appraisor/Évaluateur Canadien* 49, 1: 42. <https://secure.sauder.ubc.ca/re_creditprogram/course_resources/courses/content/452/moulton.pdf>, as of April 23, 2012.

NAFTA Secretariat (undated). North American Free Trade Agreement. <http://www.nafta-sec-alena.org/en/view.aspx?x=343&mtpilD=ALL>, as of December 23, 2011.

Newman, Warren J. (2007). Living with the Amending Procedures: Prospects for Constitutional Reform in Canada. *Supreme Court Law Review* (2007), 37 S.C.L.R. (2d). <http://www.google.ca/url?sa=t&rct=j&q=&esrc=s&source=web&cd=14&ved=0CDgQFjADOAo&url=http%3A%2F%2Fwww.droitcivil.uottawa.ca%2Findex.php%3Foption%3Dcom_docman%26task%3Ddoc_download%26gid%3D2051&ei=zWxET56PMMifiQKI_bjqDg&usg=AFQjCNEEvNQhQi4EEl2xfoadQBRt_SPOBQ&sig2=0_qOl0Q_8MlpD0twaro04A>, as of February 29, 2012.

North, Douglass (1990). *Institutions, Institutional Change and Economic Performance.* Cambridge University Press.

North, Douglass (1991). Institutions. *Journal of Economic Perspectives* 5, 1 (Winter): 97–112. <http://classwebs.spea.indiana.edu/kenricha/classes/v640/v640%20readings/north%201991.pdf>, as of November 10, 2011.

Norton, Seth W. (1998). Poverty, Property Rights, and Human Well-Being: A Cross-National Study. *Cato Journal* 18, 2 (Fall): 233–45. <http://www.cato.org/pubs/journal/cj18n2/cj18n2-4.pdf>, as of April 4, 2012.

O'Driscoll, Gerald P., Jr., and Lee Hoskins (2003). *Property Rights: The Key to Economic Development*. Policy Analysis No. 482. Cato Institute (August 7). <http://www.cato.org/pubs/pas/pa482.pdf>, as of April 4, 2012.

O'Neill, Terry (2005, October 3). Fish or Foul? BC Residents Say It's Not Fair that the Fisheries Department Has Taken Over Their Property, Especially When There's Not Even Any Water in Sight. *Western Standard*: <http://www.westernstandard.ca/website/article.php?id=1054>, as of October 17, 2011.

Pasour, E.C., Jr. (1981). The Free Rider as a Basis for Government Intervention. *Journal of Libertarian Studies* 5, 4 (Fall): 453–63.

Reid, Scott (2011). A Remedy for Property Rights Horror Stories: A Constitutional Amendment. *C2C Journal*. <http://c2cjournal.ca/2011/06/a-remedy-for-property-rights-horror-stories-a-constitutional-amendment/> as of February 29, 2012.

Reich, Charles (1964). The New Property. *Yale Law Journal* 73, 5: 733–87.

Scully, G. (1988). The Institutional Framework and Economic Development. *Journal of Political Economy* 96: 52–62.

Sharman, Campbell (1984). The Strange Case of a Provincial Constitution. *Canadian Journal of Political Science* 17, 1 (March): 87–108.

Stroup, Richard, and John Baden (1979). Property Rights and Natural Resource Management. *Literature of Liberty* 2, 4 (September-December): 5–44. <http://www.econlib.org/library/Essays/LtrLbrty/strbdPR1.html#LF-0353-1979v4-Essay01lev1sec001>, as of April 5, 2012.

Stroup, Richard (2008). Free-Market Environmentalism. *Concise Encyclopaedia of Economics*. Library of Economics and Liberty. <http://www.econlib.org/library/Enc/FreeMarketEnvironmentalism.html>, as of April 5, 2012.

Todd, E.C.E. (1992). *Law of Expropriation and Compensation in Canada*, 2nd ed. Carswell.

Tortensson, J. (1994). Property Rights and Economic Growth: An Empirical Study. *Kyklos* 47: 231–47.

Tri-City News (2005, August 24). Coquitlam is "Unfair," Say Burke residents. *Tri-City News*: 1.

Victoria Times Colonist (2005, September 22). Environmental Protection Order Leaves Property Owner Fuming. *Victoria Times Colonist*: A4.

Walker, Tony (undated). Landowners Beware! Property Rights v. Environmentalism. Presentation to the Policy Subcommittee of the Rural Summit. Goulbourn Landowners Group. <http://tiffanyweb.bmts.com/~opera/1205%20Walker%20Property%20Rights%20Submission%20_Condensed_%20_1_.pdf>, as of April 5, 2012.

Wilkinson, Bryce (2008). *A Primer on Property Rights, Takings and Compensation*. Business New Zealand, Federated Farmers, the New Zealand Business Roundtable, and the New Zealand Chambers of Commerce. <http://www.businessnz.org.nz/file/1620/081024%20Property%20rights%20Wilkinson.pdf>, as of July 6, 2011.

Wiseman, Nelson (2008). In Search of a Quebec Constitution. *Revue québécoise de droit constitutionnel* 2: 130–49. <http://www.aqdc.org/volumes/pdf/Wiseman.pdf> as of February 29, 2012.

Government sources

British Columbia (undated a). *About the Agricultural Land Reserve. Provincial Agricultural Land Commission.* Web page. Government of British Columbia. <http://www.alc.gov.bc.ca/alr/alr_main.htm>, as of November 20, 2011.

British Columbia (undated b). *Crown Land Factsheet.* BC Ministry of Agriculture and Lands. <http://www.for.gov.bc.ca/land_tenures/documents/publications/crownland_factsheet.pdf>, as of April 12, 2012.

Canada (1940). *Report of the Royal Commission on Dominion-Provincial Relations. Book I. Canada: 1867–1939.* King's Printer.

Canada (1982). Canadian Charter of Rights and Freedoms. Constitution Act, 1982. <http://laws-lois.justice.gc.ca/eng/charter/>, as of November 2, 2011.

Canada (2005). 38th Parliament, 1st Session. Hansard no. 131 (4 October 2005) at 1740 (Gordon O'Connor).

Canada (2011). Fisheries Act. Department of Justice. <http://lois-laws.justice.gc.ca/PDF/F-14.pdf>, as of October 18, 2011.

Canada (undated). *What is Intellectual Property (IP)?* Web page. Canadian Intellectual Property Office. <http://www.cipo.ic.gc.ca/eic/site/cipointernet-internetopic.nsf/eng/Home>, as of October 24, 2011.

Canada, Department of Justice (1960). Canadian Bill of Rights. <http://laws.justice.gc.ca/PDF/C-12.3.pdf>, as of November 2, 2011.

Canada, Department of Justice (undated a). *Constitution Acts, 1867 to 1982.* Web page. <http://laws-lois.justice.gc.ca/eng/Const/FullText.html>, as of November 15, 2011.

Canada, Department of Justice (undated b). *Procedure for Amending the Constitution.* <http://laws.justice.gc.ca/eng/Const/page-13.html#sc:7_IV_I>, as of November 15, 2011.

Foreign Affairs and International Trade (2012). *Negotiations and Agreements*. Web page. Government of Canada. <http://www.international. gc.ca/trade-agreements-accords-commerciaux/agr-acc/index.aspx?view=d>, as of February 26, 2012.

Ontario (2005a). Order in Council No. 208/2005. <http://www.mah. gov.on.ca/Asset1282.aspx>, as of December 18, 2011.

Ontario (2005b). *Greenbelt Plan 2005*. Ontario Ministry of Municipal Affairs and Housing. <http://www.mah.gov.on.ca/Asset1277. aspx>, as of December 18, 2011.

Ontario (2008a, May 28). *Letter to the City of Ottawa*. Ministry of Natural Resources. <http://ottawa.ca/cs/groups/content/@webottawa/ documents/pdf/mdaw/mdu0/~edisp/con035103.pdf>, as of November 30, 2011.

Ontario (2008b). *Growing the Greenbelt*. Ontario Ministry of Municipal Affairs and Housing. <http://www.mah.gov.on.ca/AssetFactory. aspx?did=5767>, as of December 18, 2011.

Ontario (2011a). *InfoSheet. Supporting the Greenbelt Plan: Planning Act Tools*. Web page. Ontario Ministry of Municipal Affairs and Housing. <http://www.mah.gov.on.ca/AssetFactory.aspx?did=7054>, as of December 18, 2011.

Ontario (2011b). *Greenbelt Protection*. Web page. Ontario Ministry of Municipal Affairs and Housing. <http://www.mah.gov.on.ca/Page187. aspx?>, as of December 18, 2011.

Privy Council Office (Undated). *The Canadian Constitution. Canadian Constitutional Amendments since 1982*. Web page. Government of Canada. <http://www.pco-bcp.gc.ca/aia/index.asp?lang=eng&page=canada&sub=c onstitution&doc=constitution-eng.htm>, as of November 15, 2011.

United States. United States Constitution. <http://www.house.gov/house/ Constitution/Constitution.html>, as of April 5, 2012.

United States, National Archives (1215/1297/2007). *Magna Carta*. Nicholas Vincent, trans. <http://www.archives.gov/exhibits/featured_ documents/magna_carta/translation.html> as of October 24, 2011.

Vancouver (1953). Vancouver Charter Amendment Act (1953). Queen's Printer. <http://www.bclaws.ca/EPLibraries/bclaws_new/document/ LOC/freeside/-%20V%20-/Vancouver%20Charter%20SBC%201953%20c.%2055/00_ Act/vanch_00.htm>, as of November 30, 2011.

Legal references

Alberta (Minister of Infrastructure) v. Nilsson, [2002] A.J. No. 1474 (C.A.), leave to appeal dismissed, [2003] S.C.C.A. No. 35.

Belfast Corporation v. O. D. Cars Ltd., (1960).

Canadian Pacific Railway Co. v. Vancouver (City), [2006] 1 S.C.R. 227, 2006 SCC 5. February 23. <http://scc.lexum.org/en/2006/2006scc5/2006scc5. html>, as of September 15, 2011.

Casimiro Resource Corp. v. British Columbia (Attorney General), (1991).

France Fenwick & Co. v. The King, [1927].

Kelo v. City of New London, 545 U.S. 469, (2005).

Manitoba Fisheries Ltd. v. The Queen, [1979] 1 S.C.R. 101. October 3, 1978. <http://scc.lexum.org/en/1978/1979scr1-101/1979scr1-101.html>, as of September 15, 2011.

Metalclad Corporation v. The United Mexican States (2000). I.L.R. 615, ICSID Case No. ARB(AF)/97/2. <http://icsid.worldbank.org/ICSID/FrontSe rvlet?requestType=CasesRH&actionVal=showDoc&docId=DC542_En&caseId=C155>, as of December 23, 2011.

Nilsson v. Alberta (1999) ABCA 340. December 1, 1999. <http://www.albertacourts.ab.ca/jdb/1998-2003/ca/Civil/1999/1999abca0340.pdf>, as of September 15, 2011.

R. v. Oakes [1986] 1 S.C.R. 103.

R. v. Tener, [1985] 1 S.C.R. 533. October 12 and 13, 1985. <http://scc.lexum.org/en/1985/1985scr1-533/1985scr1-533.html>, as of September 15, 2011.

Shamon v. Biggar (Rural Municipality No. 347) [2003] SJ. No. 347.

Supreme Court of the United States (2002). Brief of George Akerlof et al. as Amici Curiae in support of *Eldred v. Ashcroft, Attorney General,* No. 01-618.

Toronto Area Transit Operating Authority v. Dell Holdings Ltd., [1997] 1 S.C.R. 32 <http://scc.lexum.org/en/1997/1997scr1-32/1997scr1-32.html>, as of September 15, 2011.

About the author

Dr Mark Milke is a Senior Fellow at the Fraser Institute and also director of Alberta policy studies. He is the author of four books and multiple public policy papers. Mark's public policy papers include a comparison of human rights in oil-producing countries, and examinations of federal-provincial transfer payments, automobile insurance, taxpayer subsidies for political parties, the flat tax, corporate welfare, airline competition, and the Canada Pension Plan. In addition, he has also published papers with Washington D.C.-based institutes such as the American Enterprise Institute, the Competitive Enterprise Institute, the Heritage Foundation, and the Brussels-based Centre for European Studies.

Dr Milke is a frequent contributor to media debate in Canada. His columns have appeared Canada-wide in the *National Post, Toronto Star, Globe and Mail, Ottawa Citizen, Montreal Gazette, Vancouver Sun,* and *Winnipeg Free Press,* among others, as well as in the Brussels-based *European Voice.* Mark is regularly interviewed by Canadian media, including the CBC, CTV, SUN-TV, Charles Adler, and Dave Rutherford.

Dr Milke is also chairman of Canada's *Journal of Ideas—C2C Journal.ca,* an occasional lecturer in political philosophy and international relations at the University of Calgary, and a Sunday columnist for the *Calgary Herald.*

Dr Milke has a Master's degree from the University of Alberta where his thesis analyzed human rights in East Asia. He also has a Ph.D. from the University of Calgary where his doctoral dissertation analyzed the rhetoric of Canadian-American relations. He lives in Calgary and his non-policy life includes an interest in architecture and history; he is a regular hiker, skier, and runner.

Acknowledgments

Thank you to Nachum Gabler for his work on the literature on property rights, contained in an appendix in this book; to Fred McMahon, Chris Schafer, Dr Russell Brown, and Dr Rainer Knopf for their review of draft versions of this book; and also to Barry Sheridan. Thank you to the Aurea Foundation for the grant to make this work possible.

Publishing information

Distribution

These publications are available from <http://www.fraserinstitute.org> in Portable Document Format (PDF) and can be read with Adobe Acrobat® or Adobe Reader®, versions 9 or later. Adobe Reader® X, the most recent version, is available free of charge from Adobe Systems Inc. at <http://get.adobe.com/reader/>. Readers who have trouble viewing or printing our PDF files using applications from other manufacturers (e.g., Apple's Preview) should use Reader® or Acrobat®.

Ordering publications

For information about ordering the printed publications of the Fraser Institute, please contact the publications coordinator:

- e-mail: sales@fraserinstitute.org
- telephone: 604.688.0221 ext. 580 or, toll free, 1.800.665.3558 ext. 580
- fax: 604.688.8539.

Media

For media enquiries, please contact our Communications Department:

- 604.714.4582
- e-mail: communications@fraserinstitute.org.

Copyright

Date of issue

May 2012

ISBN

978-0-88975-256-6
Printed and bound in Canada.

Citation

Milke, Mark (2012). *Stealth Confiscation: How Governments Regulate, Freeze And Devalue Private Property—without Compensation.* Fraser Institute. <http://www.fraserinstitute.org>.

Editing

Kristin McCahon

Typesetting and design

Lindsey Thomas Martin

Cover design and artwork

Bill C. Ray

Images for cover

Rural landscape of Farm © dplett (Bigstock)
Reaching hand © Maikes (Bigstock)
Tall buildings © Milke

Supporting the Fraser Institute

To learn how to support the Fraser Institute, please contact

- Development Department, Fraser Institute
  Fourth Floor, 1770 Burrard Street
  Vancouver, British Columbia, V6J 3G7 Canada
- telephone, toll-free: 1.800.665.3558 ext. 586
- e-mail: development@fraserinstitute.org

Lifetime patrons

For their long-standing and valuable support contributing to the success of the Fraser Institute, the following people have been recognized and inducted as Lifetime Patrons of the Fraser Institute.

Sonja Bata	Serge Darkazanli	Fred Mannix
Charles Barlow	John Dobson	Con Riley
Ev Berg	Raymond Heung	Catherine Windels
Art Grunder	Bill Korol	
Jim Chaplin	Bill Mackness	

Purpose, funding, & independence

The Fraser Institute provides a useful public service. We report objective information about the economic and social effects of current public policies, and we offer evidence-based research and education about policy options that can improve the quality of life.

The Institute is a non-profit organization. Our activities are funded by charitable donations, unrestricted grants, ticket sales, and sponsorships from events, the licensing of products for public distribution, and the sale of publications.

All research is subject to rigorous review by external experts, and is conducted and published separately from the Institute's Board of Trustees and its donors.

The opinions expressed by the authors of our publications are those of the individuals themselves, and do not necessarily reflect those of the Institute, its Board of Trustees, its donors and supporters, or its staff. This publication in no way implies that the Fraser Institute, its trustees, or staff are in favour of, or oppose the passage of, any bill; or that they support or oppose any particular political party or candidate.

As a healthy part of public discussion among fellow citizens who desire to improve the lives of people through better public policy, the Institute welcomes evidence-focused scrutiny of the research we publish, including verification of data sources, replication of analytical methods, and intelligent debate about the practical effects of policy recommendations.

About the Fraser Institute

Our vision is a free and prosperous world where individuals benefit from greater choice, competitive markets, and personal responsibility. Our mission is to measure, study, and communicate the impact of competitive markets and government interventions on the welfare of individuals.

Founded in 1974, we are an independent Canadian research and educational organization with locations throughout North America and international partners in over 85 countries. Our work is financed by tax-deductible contributions from thousands of individuals, organizations, and foundations. In order to protect its independence, the Institute does not accept grants from government or contracts for research.

Nous envisageons un monde libre et prospère, où chaque personne bénéficie d'un plus grand choix, de marchés concurrentiels et de responsabilités individuelles. Notre mission consiste à mesurer, à étudier et à communiquer l'effet des marchés concurrentiels et des interventions gouvernementales sur le bien-être des individus.

Peer review

Validating the accuracy of our research

The Fraser Institute maintains a rigorous peer review process for its research. New research, major research projects, and substantively modified research conducted by the Fraser Institute are reviewed by a minimum of one internal expert and two external experts. Reviewers are expected to have a recognized expertise in the topic area being addressed. Whenever possible, external review is a blind process.

Commentaries and conference papers are reviewed by internal experts. Updates to previously reviewed research or new editions of previously reviewed research are not reviewed unless the update includes substantive or material changes in the methodology.

The review process is overseen by the directors of the Institute's research departments who are responsible for ensuring all research published by the Institute passes through the appropriate peer review. If a dispute about the recommendations of the reviewers should arise during the Institute's peer review process, the Institute has an Editorial Advisory Board, a panel of scholars from Canada, the United States, and Europe to whom it can turn for help in resolving the dispute.

Editorial Advisory Board